ICE CREAMS AND SORBETS

Edited by
Wendy James and Gill Edden

Galley Press

The material in this book has previously
appeared in *The Complete Cook*

© EDIPEM, Novara 1976
© 1978, 1979, 1980, 1981, 1984
Orbis Publishing, London

Published in this edition 1984 by Galley Press,
an imprint of W. H. Smith and Son Limited,
Registered No. 237811 England.
Trading as WHS Distributors, St John's House,
East Street, Leicester, LE1 6NE

Printed in Spain
ISBN 0 86136 864 9
by Grijelmo S.A. Bilbao

Contents

Ice creams and sorbets

Rich and creamy, or cold and sharp, ices make perfect desserts.
They can also be served as starters or as between meal snacks.
For true luxury, make your own ice creams and sorbets, experimenting
with flavours to your heart's content. For quick desserts, dress up
commercial ices to make tantalizing treats.

Economical ice cream

The use of evaporated milk rather than cream means this ice cream is relatively cheap to make. It isn't as rich as the basic vanilla ice and is therefore recommended as a base for strong flavourings

DESSERT   Makes 1½ pints (850ml)

Overall timing 30 minutes plus freezing

Equipment 3 bowls, saucepan, freezer tray or rigid container

Freezing Freeze in tray and cover. Freezer life: 2 months. To use: soften in fridge for 30 minutes before serving

INGREDIENTS

14½oz	Can of evaporated milk	411g
1 teasp	Powdered gelatine	5ml
3 tbsp	Water	3×15ml
3oz	Caster sugar	75g
1 teasp	Vanilla essence	5ml

METHOD
1 Chill evaporated milk. Sprinkle the gelatine on to the water in a small bowl and leave until spongy. Stand bowl in a pan of simmering water and stir until gelatine dissolves. Cool slightly.
2 Whisk the evaporated milk, sugar and vanilla essence in a bowl until thick and foamy, then whisk in gelatine.
3 Pour mixture into freezer tray and freeze until mushy.
4 Remove mixture from freezer and turn into a large bowl. Whisk until almost doubled in bulk. Return to freezer tray and freeze until solid.

Low-fat ice cream

Made from diabetic jelly sweetened with saccharine, fruit yogurt and skimmed milk, this is a good recipe for slimmers who have to forego the calorie-packed, rich ice creams. It's more like a water ice than a true ice cream, but will satisfy cravings

DESSERT   Makes 1½ pints (850ml)

Overall timing 20 minutes plus about 2 hours freezing

Equipment 4 bowls, saucepan, freezer tray or rigid container

Freezing Freeze in tray and cover. Freezer life: 2 months. To use: soften in fridge for 30 minutes before serving

INGREDIENTS

1	Diabetic jelly	1
1lb	Carton of fruit yogurt	450g
3 tbsp	Skimmed milk powder	3×15ml
½ pint	Water	300ml
1	Egg	1

METHOD
1 Put jelly crystals and a little water in a bowl. Place over a pan of hot water and stir until dissolved. Allow to cool slightly then beat in the yogurt. Make up milk by mixing the skimmed milk powder with the water.
2 Separate the egg. Whisk the egg yolk till light in colour, then beat into the jelly and yogurt mixture. Beat in the milk.
3 Pour into freezer tray and freeze until mushy (about 20 minutes).

4 Remove tray from freezer, turn ice in bowl and beat well. Whisk egg wh[ite] till stiff, then fold into mixture. Retu[rn] to freezer tray and freeze till fi[rm] (about 1½ hours).

Above: an electrical ice cream maker save[s] beating by hand and gives a creamier mix[ture]

time saver

Electrical ice cream makers save you both time and energy (though not fuel). Because the blades or paddles go on moving during the freezing process, the results are creamier and the bulk increases because the movement aerates the mixture too. There are various types available, and although they all work well the less fiddly ones have paddles that lift automatically before the freezing cream traps them.
With other types you have to remove the paddles before the ice cream sets hard. The machines have a flat flex so freezer or fridge doors can close flat without denting the seal.

asic vanilla
ce cream

rich, creamy yellow ice made from custard base. The added cream creases the fat content and gives e mixture a wonderfully smooth xture. It is beaten twice at the lf-frozen stage so that the ice ystals are broken down

SSERT Makes 1 pint (560ml)

erall timing 40 minutes plus freezing

uipment 3 bowls, 2 saucepans, sieve d muslin, freezer tray or mould

eezing Freeze in tray or mould, or ke scoops and arrange on plastic tray, en cover, label and refreeze. Freezer : 2 months. To use: soften before ving by placing tray or mould in lge for 30 minutes, scoops on tray minutes

GREDIENTS

z	Egg yolks	2
pint	Caster sugar	50g
	Milk	300ml
	Vanilla pod *or*	1
teasp	Vanilla essence	5ml
pint	Carton of double cream	150ml

ETHOD

Put the egg yolks and sugar in a large bowl and beat until creamy.
Put milk and vanilla pod or essence into a pan and bring to just under boiling point. Remove from heat and take out vanilla pod if used.
Pour milk in a thin stream on to creamed mixture, stirring continuously. Place bowl over a pan of simmering water and cook for about 10 minutes without boiling, stirring continuously until mixture coats the back of the spoon.
Remove from heat and strain through a muslin-lined sieve into a bowl. Beat until cool to prevent skin forming.
Whisk the cream until it just holds its shape, then fold into cold custard. Pour into freezer tray or mould and freeze for about 1½ hours or until mushy.
Turn ice cream into a bowl and beat well. Pour back into container and return to freezer. Freeze till mushy.
Repeat beating process, then return to freezer and freeze till firm.

Above: Basic vanilla ice served in scoops. For flavouring suggestions, see page 6

1 *Put the egg yolks and sugar into a bowl and beat with a wooden spoon until creamy*

2 *Put milk and vanilla pod into a saucepan and bring to just under boiling point*

3 *Pour hot milk on to creamed mix in a thin stream, stirring continuously, then cook*

4 *Strain custard, beat until cool, fold in whipped cream. Pour into tray or mould*

5

Flavourings for ice creams

Until you've tried making your own ice creams at home, you won't realize just how much better they are than the commercial ones. What's more, you can have fun experimenting with all the different flavourings you can add — everything from exotic pawpaw to brown breadcrumbs. All the suggestions given here can be added to the Basic vanilla ice or the Economical ice cream recipes on pages 4 and 5. Most of the flavourings are added to the basic mix before it's poured into the freezer container and put into the freezer for the first time; some can be added to the milk if you're making the custard-based ice cream

Chocolate

Add 2oz (50g) melted plain or milk chocolate. If making the vanilla ice cream recipe, the chocolate can be melted in the hot milk before the custard is made.
Variations: Flavour with chocolate as above and add 2oz (50g) chopped nuts. Or, flavour with 2oz (50g) chocolate dots or 2oz (50g) grated or finely chopped peppermint-flavoured chocolate bar.

Coffee

Dissolve 2 teasp (2×5ml) instant coffee in a little hot water and stir into ice cream mixture, or use 2 teasp (2×5ml) liquid coffee. Add 1 tbsp (15ml) Tia Maria or other liqueur. If making the vanilla ice cream, the coffee can be dissolved in the hot milk if preferred.

Below: Praline ice cream — continental style with crisp and crunchy toffee bits

Crunchy

Make a half quantity of praline accordi to instructions on page 16. Crush in small pieces with a rolling-pin and into the ice cream mixture.
Variations: Add 4oz (125g) crushed p nut brittle, almond toffee or peppermi rock. Alternatively, replace 1oz (25g) the sugar in the basic recipe with ma syrup and add 2oz (50g) chopped walnu For pistachio ice cream, add ½ teasp (2.5 pistachio flavouring or peppermint esser and 2oz (50g) shelled and chopped pis chio nuts (not salted ones).
For brown bread ice cream, spread 2 (50g) fresh brown breadcrumbs on baki tray and sprinkle with 1oz (25g) cas sugar. Bake at 350F (180C) Gas 4 for minutes, stirring frequently, until cri Cool completely, then stir into basic m

Preserved fruits

To make tutti-frutti ice cream, add 4 (125g) chopped glacé or candied fruit the basic mixture.
For a rum and raisin flavour, soak 3 (75g) plump seedless raisins in 2 tl (2×15ml) hot rum. Cool, stir into mixtu

Soft fruits

Wash and hull either 8oz (225g) r strawberries, raspberries, blackberries loganberries (or use frozen, unsweeten fruit). Purée in a blender, then rub throu a sieve to remove seeds. Fold into ba mixture with 2oz (50g) caster sugar. liked, add 1 tbsp (15ml) orange liqueur Kirsch. Drained canned fruit can be sub tuted, but extra sugar will not be require Soft fruits such as blackcurrants, re currants or gooseberries need to be cook before adding them to the basic ice crea mix. Wash and top and tail 8oz (225 fruit. Simmer in 2 tbsp (2×15ml) wa with 2oz (50g) caster sugar until tend Cool. Purée fruit and cooking juices in blender, then rub through a sieve befo adding to basic mixture. If you like, or sugar and use drained and sieved cann fruit of choice.

Top fruits

Peel 8oz (225g) apricots, peaches or pea and remove stones. Chop flesh and pur in a blender with 1 tbsp (15ml) lemon jui or rub through a sieve. Stir into basic mi ture with 2oz (50g) caster sugar. If usi drained, canned fruit, do not add suga

xotic fruits

el and finely chop 8oz (225g) fresh
eapple or drain a 15½oz (439g) can of
ished pineapple. If using fresh fruit,
x with 2oz (50g) caster sugar. Fold into
sic mixture.

r a banana flavour, peel and mash 2
ge, ripe not brown, bananas and mix
th 2 tbsp (2×15ml) lemon juice. Stir
to the basic mixture.

el a ripe mango weighing about 12oz
50g). Remove stone and rub flesh
rough a sieve or chop finely. Stir into
e basic mixture with 2oz (50g) caster
gar.

ain a 15oz (425g) can of guavas. Rub
lp through a sieve and add to basic

ice cream mixture.

Halve 1 ripe pawpaw, scoop out and
discard seeds. Remove flesh and mash
with 2oz (50g) caster sugar and the juice
of 1 lime. Stir into basic mixture.

Scoop flesh out of 1 ripe avocado and
mash with 1 teasp (5ml) lemon juice and
2oz (50g) caster sugar. Stir into ice
cream with 1oz (25g) shelled and chopped
pistachio nuts, and a few drops of green
food colouring if liked.

Cut open 6 ripe passionfruit and scoop
out the flesh. Rub through a sieve, then
mix juice with 2oz (50g) caster sugar and
a few drops of yellow food colouring if
liked. Stir into basic ice cream mix.

A few ice cream recipes appear in
18th century cookery books but it
wasn't until the middle of the 19th
century that interest increased
because of the invention of home
ice making machines in the United
States. The Americans still have the
taste and today eat more ice cream
per head than any other nation —
with a reputed 200 flavours!

*Below: from the Caribbean, three exotic
ice creams flavoured with pineapple, mango
and guava. Serve in hollowed out pineapple
shells and surround with ice cubes to keep
the ice cream from melting*

To give citrus water ices extra flavour, add finely pared rind (be careful not to remove bitter pith) to the sugar syrup

When the fruit juice has been added, strain mixture into freezer tray to make a water ice, or granita

Basic water ice

The most refreshing of desserts, water ices are simple to make and are useful freezer standbys. The same principle can be used for delectable starters, too – see page 9. To make sherbets and sorbets, see the captions, right

DESSERT   Serves 6

Overall timing 20 minutes plus freezing

Equipment Saucepan, sieve, 2 pint (1.1 litre) freezer tray, 2 bowls

Freezing Freeze in tray. Freezer life: 6 months. To use: serve from frozen

INGREDIENTS

8oz	Caster sugar	225g
1 pint	Water	560ml
1/4 pint	Fruit juice	150ml

Above: Lemon sherbet – a basic water ice which has been made fluffy with the addition of a softly whisked egg white. To make lemon granita, leave out the egg white, and to make a sorbet, see right

METHOD
1 Put the sugar and water in a pan and heat slowly, stirring until sugar dissolves. Bring to the boil and simmer for 10 minutes without stirring – do not let it colour. Remove from heat and leave to cool.
2 Add fruit juice to syrup, strain into freezer tray and freeze until mushy.
3 Remove mixture from freezer, turn into a bowl and beat well to break down crystals. Return to freezer tray and freeze till firm.

To make a sherbet, *remove mixture from freezer when mushy, turn into bowl and beat well. Whisk 1 egg white till soft peaks form, then fold into beaten mix. Freeze till firm, then serve*
To make a sorbet, *whisk 2 egg whites and proceed as for sherbet. To give a very soft texture, make the sorbet with gelatine which prevents the formation of ice crystals. Sprinkle 2 teasp (2×5ml) of powdered gelatine over 2 tbsp (2×15ml) water, wine or liqueur in a cup and leave to sponge. After syrup has simmered for 10 minutes, add the soaked gelatine and stir till dissolved. Freeze till mushy, then beat. Whisk 2 egg whites till stiff, then whisk into beaten mixture. Cover, freeze till firm*
To freeze sorbets in shells *(see picture page 28), make the syrup adding gelatine as above. Fold whisked whites into beaten mixture, then pile into shells, pack into rigid container, cover and freeze*

Flavourings for water ices

Savoury water ices make unusual and refreshing starters — excellent for the summer. The sweet ices are made from the basic recipe, page 8

Creamy avocado ice

Cut 2 small ripe avocados in half, remove stones and scoop out flesh into a bowl. Rub insides of shells with lemon juice and reserve. Mash avocado flesh with ¼ pint (150ml) soured cream, then mix in 1 tbsp (15ml) lemon juice, ½ teasp (2.5ml) French mustard and 1 tbsp (15ml) finely chopped chives. Put into freezer tray and freeze until mushy. Remove from freezer, beat well and add seasoning to taste. Return to freezer until set. Allow to soften in the fridge for 30 minutes before serving in reserved shells.

Cider and cucumber sorbet

Peel a large cucumber and cut into dice. Put 1 tbsp (15ml) water and 1 teasp (5ml) powdered gelatine in a cup and leave to sponge. Place in hot water and stir until gelatine dissolves. Cool slightly, then stir into ½ pint (300ml) cider. Add 2 tbsp (2×15ml) lemon juice and the cucumber pieces. Purée mixture in a blender, taste and season. Put into freezer tray and freeze until mushy. Remove from freezer, beat well, taste and adjust seasoning, then fold in 2 softly whisked egg whites. Freeze until firm. Soften in fridge 15 minutes before using. Scoop out of tray with a melon baller and serve in small chilled glasses garnished with sprigs of mint.

Tomato and orange ice

Slice the tops off 4 oranges. Remove orange flesh and press through sieve to remove juice. Make up to ½ pint (300ml) with water if necessary. Reserve orange shells. Boil 4oz (125g) caster sugar with the orange juice for 5 minutes. Allow to cool, then stir in ¾ pint (400ml) tomato juice and 1 tbsp (15ml) lemon juice. Season. Pour into freezer tray and freeze until mushy. Remove from freezer, beat well, then taste and adjust seasoning. Divide mixture between reserved shells. Brush outside of oranges with water — this will give an attractive frosted look — and return them to the freezer until firm. Soften in fridge 15 minutes before serving. Garnish with sprigs of basil or mint.

Fruity water ice

Make basic syrup and substitute ¼ pint (150ml) fruit purée and 1 tbsp (15ml) lemon juice for the fruit juice.

Champagne sorbet

Make basic syrup and substitute ¼ pint (150ml) champagne or dry cider and 1 tbsp (15ml) lemon juice for the fruit juice. Fold in 2 whisked egg whites.

Below: Champagne sorbet — a light, fluffy textured dessert that makes a stylish end for a dinner party. Serve in individual coupes with langue de chat biscuits

Above: French parfait – refreshingly cool

French parfait

A simply made ice that doesn't have to be stirred during freezing

DESSERT Makes 1 pint (560ml)

Overall timing 30 minutes plus chilling and freezing

Equipment Saucepan, 2 bowls, electric whisk, freezer tray

Freezing Freeze in tray and cover. Freezer life: 2 months. To use: soften in fridge for 30 minutes before serving

INGREDIENTS

¼ pint	Water	150ml
2oz	Caster sugar	50g
1	Vanilla pod	1
4	Egg yolks	4
½ pint	Carton of double cream	284ml

METHOD

1 Put the water and sugar into a pan and stir over a low heat until sugar dissolves. Add the vanilla pod and boil gently for 5 minutes. Remove from heat, take out vanilla pod and cool slightly.

2 Place egg yolks in a bowl and beat with an electric whisk until pale and thick. While still beating, trickle in the syrup in a thin stream. Continue whisking until mixture is cool. Chill in fridge for 30 minutes.

3 Whisk cream to soft peaks and fold into the yolk mixture. Pour into freezer tray and freeze till firm. Serve in individual glasses with Tuiles (see page 41).

VARIATION

To make a liqueur-flavoured parfait, omit the vanilla pod and add 4 tbsp (4×15ml) liqueur when you fold the cream into the chilled mixture.

Fruit mousse

Whisked egg whites lighten this rich cream and puréed fruit mixture

DESSERT Makes 1½ pints (850ml)

Overall timing 15 minutes plus chilling and freezing

Equipment Blender, sieve, 3 bowls, freezer tray or rigid container

Freezing Freeze in tray and cover. Freezer life: 2 months. To use: soften in fridge for 30 minutes before serving

INGREDIENTS

12oz	Fresh or stewed fruit (strawberries, raspberries, peaches, plums, blackcurrants)	350g
1–2oz	Caster sugar	25–50g
1–2 tbsp	Lemon juice	1 or 2 ×15ml
½ pint	Carton of double cream	284ml
3	Egg whites	3

METHOD

1 Purée the fruit in a blender and if necessary press through a sieve to remove seeds. Add sugar and lemon juice and chill for 30 minutes.

2 Whisk cream until soft peaks form. Fold into fruit purée. Whisk egg whites till stiff but not dry and gently fold into the mixture with a metal spoon.

3 Pour mixture into freezer tray or container and freeze till firm.

VARIATION

To make chocolate mousse, melt 4oz (125g) plain dessert chocolate with 2 tbsp (2×15ml) caster sugar and 4 tbsp (4×15 ml) water in a bowl placed over a pan of simmering water. Allow to cool, then fold into mixture before freezing.

Zuccotto

The Italians are not over fond of hot, heavy puddings. Instead, they prefer fruit, ice cream or sponge cakes. In this recipe, all three are combined to make a glorious sponge-lined bombe. There is some dispute over the origin of the term zuccotto — some say it refers to the amount of sugar (zucchero) in the dessert; while others believe that the literal translation of the word — skullcap — refers to the finished shape. Whatever the case, this rich, liqueur-flavoured dessert is well worth trying

Line base and sides of mould with sponge cake pieces, then sprinkle with liqueur

Spoon softened ice creams into the mould and smooth surface. Cover with sponge

Right: Zuccotto — liqueur-flavoured sponge mould filled with ice cream. If you like, use Fruit mousse (recipe left) for the second layer rather than tutti-frutti ice cream

DESSERT   Serves 6–8

Overall timing 1¾ hours

Equipment 2 pint (1.1 litre) mould or pudding basin

Freezing Freeze in basin and cover. Freezer life: 2 months. To use: soften in fridge for 30 minutes before serving

INGREDIENTS

pint	Chocolate and nut ice cream	560ml
pint	Tutti-frutti ice cream	560ml
oz	Sponge cake	225g
tbsp	Liqueur	2×15ml

METHOD

Remove both ice creams from freezer and leave in fridge to soften for about 20 minutes. The ice cream should be soft enough to work with, but not runny. Cut cake into thin slices. Use three quarters of the cake to line the base and sides of the mould. Sprinkle sponge with liqueur (any kind would do, but Curaçao, Cognac or Kirsch would complement the ice cream flavours). Working quickly, spoon softened chocolate and nut ice cream into sponge-lined mould and smooth surface. Top with tutti-frutti ice cream, smooth surface and cover with remaining sponge pieces. Cover and freeze till firm.

TO SERVE

Transfer mould to fridge 30 minutes before serving. Run a knife around the edge to loosen and turn out on to a chilled serving dish. Decorate with whipped cream and glacé cherries if liked.

Cassata gelata

An Italian speciality, a cassata consists of layers of different flavoured ice creams frozen in a mould. It's important to get the consistency of the ice creams just right so you can spread them against the sides of the mould with a spoon

DESSERT   Serves 8

Overall timing 1¾ hours

Equipment 2½ pint (1.5 litre) bombe mould or pudding basin

Freezing Freeze in mould or basin. Freezer life: 2 months. To use: soften in fridge for 20 minutes before serving

INGREDIENTS

1 pint	Vanilla ice cream	560ml
1 pint	Chocolate ice cream	560ml
½ pint	Tutti-frutti ice cream	300ml

Above: Cassata gelata – serve in slices

METHOD

1 Chill mould. Remove vanilla ice cream from freezer and soften in fridge for 15–20 minutes. Spoon two-thirds of the vanilla ice cream into the mould, pressing it firmly to cover shape of mould. Place remaining vanilla ice cream and mould in freezer and leave till firm. Meanwhile, remove chocolate ice cream from freezer and leave to soften in fridge.

2 Take mould out of freezer and press in layer of chocolate ice cream following shape of mould and leaving space in middle. Return mould to freezer for 20 minutes. Meanwhile, remove remaining vanilla ice cream from freezer and leave to soften in fridge.

3 Spread over chocolate layer, leaving space in middle, and return to freezer for 20 minutes. Meanwhile, remove tutti-frutti ice cream from freezer and soften in fridge.

4 Remove mould from freezer and fill centre with tutti-frutti ice cream. Smooth surface. Cover with lid or foil and freeze till firm.

TO SERVE

Place mould in fridge for 30 minutes. Dip mould in hot water for a few seconds to loosen ice cream. Turn out on to plate.

Fruity ice creams

Two impressive different ice creams, and although one cheats a little, both are special because of the added fruits. Let them soften at room temperature for about 10 minutes before serving

Glace plombières

A French mixture that unifies bought ice cream, jam and fruit

DESSERT Serves 6–8

Overall timing 15 minutes plus maceration and freezing

Equipment 2lb (900g) loaf tin, 2 bowls

Freezing See Method

Above: Glace plombières
Below: beat macerated fruits into ice cream

Below: fill centre of lined tin with jam, top with rest of ice cream, then freeze

INGREDIENTS

4oz	Chopped candied fruit	125g
4 tbsp	Apricot brandy	4×15ml
1¾ pints	Non-dairy vanilla ice cream	1 litre
8oz	Apricot jam	225g

METHOD

1 Put the loaf tin in the freezer or freezing compartment of the fridge. Place glacé fruit in a bowl, add apricot brandy and leave to macerate for 30 minutes.
2 Put ice cream into a bowl, add fruit and liqueur and quickly mix well with a wooden spoon.
3 Remove tin from freezer and coat base and sides with a thick layer of the ice cream mixture.
4 Spoon jam into the centre of the tin, then cover with remaining ice cream. Smooth surface with a wetted knife and place in freezer for at least 2 hours. Turn out of tin and cut into slices to serve.

VARIATION

Put 4oz (125g) chopped candied fruit in a bowl with 2 tbsp (2×15ml) Kirsch and leave to macerate for 30 minutes. Whisk 4fl oz (113ml) carton of double cream in a bowl till stiff peaks form, then mix into softened ice cream, together with the drained fruit. Spoon ice cream into a dampened mould, cover with foil and freeze till firm. To serve, turn out on to a serving plate and decorate with piped rosettes of whipped cream. Place a glacé cherry in the centre of each rosette and arrange more glacé cherries round the ice cream. Serve at once.

Festive ice cream

Whatever the weather at Christmas, a fruity ice cream is a splendid way to finish a heavy meal

DESSERT Serves 6–8

Overall timing 30 minutes plus overnight maceration and freezing

Equipment Saucepan, 3 bowls, freezer tray or pudding basin

Freezing See Method

INGREDIENTS

6oz	Dried fruit (apricots, peaches, raisins, sultanas, dates)	175g
4 tbsp	Brandy or rum	4×15ml
¾ pint	Milk	400ml
1	Stick of cinnamon	1
3	Eggs	3
4oz	Caster sugar	125g
¾ pint	Double or whipping cream	400ml

METHOD

1 Finely chop the dried fruit and place i a bowl, cover with brandy or rum an leave to macerate overnight.
2 The next day, put the milk and cinna mon stick into a pan. Bring to the boi then remove from the heat and leav to infuse for 10 minutes. Remov cinnamon stick.
3 Beat the eggs and sugar together in bowl. Pour in the milk, stirring. Retur to pan and cook, stirring, over a gentl heat until the custard thickens. Remov from heat and leave to cool.
4 Whip the cream in a bowl till stiff. Fol in the cooled custard, then the drie fruit, brandy or rum.
5 Turn mixture into freezer tray o pudding basin and freeze till mushy
6 Remove from freezer and turn mixtur into a bowl. Stir well to make sure th fruit is well distributed. Return t freezer tray or basin, smooth surfac with a wetted palette knife and freez till firm.
7 Remove from the refrigerator 1 minutes before ready to serve, the turn out on to serving plate an decorate with whipped cream.

eezer dessert

nelt-in-the-mouth dessert

SSERT		Serves 6

erall timing 10 minutes plus freezing

uipment Bowl, freezer tray

ezing See Method

GREDIENTS

int	Double cream	400ml
ž	Caster sugar	75g
ž	Dried mixed fruit	125g
ž	Chopped nuts	50g
ž	Chopped glacé cherries	50g

THOD

Whip the cream and sugar in a bowl till thick. Add the dried fruit, nuts and cherries and mix thoroughly.
Turn the mixture into freezer tray and freeze for 1–2 hours until firm. Remove from freezer 10 minutes before serving. Serve with crisp wafer biscuits.

Coupes glacées aux raisins

This dessert combines home-made vanilla ice cream with grapes and a port sauce to make a really special end to a meal. To save time, use ready-made Italian-style ice cream, add fresh grapes and spoon sauce over

DESSERT		Serves 4

Overall timing 45 minutes plus freezing

Equipment 2 bowls, 2 saucepans, freezer tray, 4 glass serving dishes

Freezing Ice cream only may be frozen, see Method

INGREDIENTS

1lb	Seedless grapes	450g
¼ pint	Port	150ml
½ pint	Milk	300ml
½ teasp	Vanilla essence	2.5ml
4	Egg yolks	4
6oz	Caster sugar	175g
	Grated rind of 1 lemon	

METHOD

1 Put the grapes in a bowl, cover with the port and leave to macerate.
2 Put the milk and vanilla into a pan and bring to the boil. Remove from heat.
3 Whisk 2 of the egg yolks in a bowl. Gradually add 2oz (50g) of the sugar and whisk till frothy. Stir in the hot milk.
4 Place bowl over a pan of simmering water and stir until custard coats the back of the spoon.
5 Turn mixture into freezer tray and freeze till firm, preferably overnight.
6 Beat together the remaining egg yolks, sugar and lemon rind till frothy. Drain port from grapes and add to bowl. Place over a pan of simmering water and whisk over a gentle heat till mixture thickens. Remove from heat and leave to cool (not in the fridge).
7 Remove ice cream from freezer, leave to soften for a few minutes, then divide between serving glasses. Arrange grapes on top and spoon port mixture over.

Below: Coupes glacées aux raisins

Above: Banana split — each serving includes a whole banana, scoops of ice cream, fruit, sauce, cream and tiny, ready-made meringues

Banana split

A delicious dessert which gets its name from the way the banana is cut

DESSERT   Serves 4

Overall timing 30 minutes

Equipment 3 mixing bowls, piping bag

Freezing Not recommended

INGREDIENTS

8oz	Strawberries*	225g
4oz	Grapes	125g
1	Orange	1
1	Kiwi fruit	1
4 tbsp	Milk shake syrup	4×15ml
2 teasp	Arrowroot (optional)	2×5ml
¼ pint	Carton of double cream	150ml
4	Bananas	4
1	Small block of vanilla ice cream	1
8	Little meringues	8

METHOD

1 Hull strawberries and cut them in half. Halve grapes and remove pips. Peel orange (be careful to remove pith) and divide into segments. Peel and slice kiwi fruit. Place all the fruits in a bowl, and put in fridge for 15 minutes.

2 Remove fruits from fridge — they should be really cold. If milk shake syrup is not thick enough, mix arrowroot with a little hot water and blend into syrup over gentle heat to thicken it. Whip cream to piping consistency.

3 Peel bananas. "Split" in half lengthways and place halves down each side of 4 serving dishes.

4 Arrange fruit between bananas and place scoops of ice cream on top. Pour over a little syrup, pipe on cream swirls and top with meringues. Serve immediately with crisp fan wafers.

* This is a recipe that can be adapted to the time of year because you can use canned fruit when the selection of fresh is not large. Make the sweet sauce from the syrup in the can, using arrowroot to thicken it and a little red food colouring.

cook's know-how

Dried bananas are a convenient form of the fruit and can be used in any recipe where the firm texture of the fresh fruit is not required. Well-packed, they have quite a long shelf life, but should be used up quickly once the pack is opened. Dried bananas are a rich source of natural sugar. They come from tropical America where they are allowed to tree-ripen, so the sugar is fully developed, then picked, peeled, selected and dried on racks in the tropical heat — but shaded from the intense sun. Finely chopped dried bananas add an interesting accent to a variety of dishes. They make a sweet topping for breakfast cereals and curries and a few pieces are delicious in salads — with celery and mushrooms for example. They can also be used in cakes, breads or puddings in place of, or as well as, other dried fruit. In casseroles and stews, too, they will make a difference to the flavour.

afé liégeois

om Liège in Belgium, this is a
nderfully cooling sundae made
m coffee ice cream and lashings
whipped cream. For extra special
casions, spoon a little Tia Maria
rum over the ice cream before
ding the piped decoration. To
joy this dessert at its best,
ke sure that all the ingredients
d the glasses are chilled

SSERT Serves 4

erall timing 15 minutes

uipment Bowl, 4 tall glasses, piping
g with star nozzle

eezing Not recommended

GREDIENTS

oz	Carton of double cream	227ml
tbsp	Milk	2×15ml
easp	Vanilla essence	1.25ml
	Scoops of coffee ice cream	4
	Sugar coffee beans	4

METHOD
1 The cream and milk must be very cold.
   Put them in a bowl with the vanilla
   essence and whisk to a piping consistency. Chill in fridge till ready to use.
2 Divide ice cream between serving
   glasses. Spoon the cream mixture into
   the piping bag, fitted with a star nozzle,
   and pipe a large swirl on top of each
   glass. Decorate with sugar coffee beans
   and serve immediately.

Creamy milk shakes

Made in a blender, these frothy
drinks are a good way to encourage
the family to enjoy milk. Experiment
with different combinations of fruit
purée and ice cream flavours, or try
adding extra pieces of chopped
fruit. The fruit purée can also be
replaced by one of the commercially
produced fruit syrups

DRINK Serves 4

Overall timing 5 minutes

Equipment Blender, 4 tall glasses

Freezing Not recommended

INGREDIENTS

½ pint	Fresh, frozen or canned fruit purée (strawberry, raspberry, banana, pineapple, peach)	300ml
	Caster sugar	
2–3	Scoops of vanilla ice cream	2–3
½ pint	Milk	300ml

METHOD
1 Sweeten fruit purée to taste. Put into
   blender with remaining ingredients and
   blend until thick and frothy.
2 Pour mixture into chilled glasses and
   serve immediately with straws.

VARIATIONS
Change the flavour of the ice cream – for
example, use chocolate or any of the
smooth-textured ice creams. Add 1 tbsp
(15ml) malted milk to the blender with
the other ingredients.

Knickerbocker glory

A glorious tribute to the early
Dutch settlers in New York. Layers
of ice cream, fruit and whipped
cream are splendidly displayed in
tall sundae glasses

DESSERT Serves 4

Overall timing 10 minutes

Equipment 4 tall sundae glasses, bowl

Freezing Not recommended

INGREDIENTS

8oz	Strawberries or raspberries	225g
¼ pint	Carton of double cream	150ml
15oz	Can of fruit cocktail	425g
	Vanilla ice cream	
	Fan wafers (optional)	

METHOD
1 Chill the sundae glasses. Wash and
   hull fruit. Whip cream in a bowl until
   stiff. Drain canned fruit.
2 Reserve a few strawberries or raspberries for decoration. Divide the rest
   between the glasses and add 2 scoops
   of ice cream to each. Cover with the
   drained fruit cocktail, then with another
   layer of ice cream. Pipe or spoon whipped cream on top and decorate with
   reserved fruit and wafers if liked. Serve
   immediately with long handled spoons.

low: Café liégeois – a thick and luscious Belgian dessert flavoured with coffee

Cherry layer dessert

An extremely rich dessert typical of Austria and parts of Germany where cherries are used in many different ways. Here they are layered with a thick mix of cream, cream cheese and liqueur

DESSERT Serves 4–6

Overall timing 15 minutes

Equipment 2 bowls, 4 to 6 serving glasses

Freezing Not recommended

INGREDIENTS

1½lb	Can of cherries	700g
3oz	Icing sugar	75g
2 tbsp	Maraschino or Kirsch	2×15ml
4oz	Cream cheese	125g
8fl oz	Carton of double cream	227ml
	Vanilla ice cream	

METHOD

1 Drain cherries and save juice. Put cherries in a bowl and sprinkle with a little of the icing sugar.
2 In another bowl, mix together 4 tbsp (4×15ml) of the reserved cherry juice, 1 tbsp (15ml) of icing sugar and the Maraschino or Kirsch. Divide between serving glasses.
3 In a bowl, mash the cream cheese with a fork. Blend in the cream and remaining icing sugar, then whip until thick.
4 Layer the cream and cherries in the glasses and top each with a cube of ice cream.

VARIATION

If you don't have any liqueur in the store-cupboard, add 4 drops of almond essence to the cream mixture.

Praline

TOFFEE OR CAKE DECORATION

Overall timing 25 minutes cooking plus cooling time

Equipment Saucepan, 2 baking trays

Freezing Not recommended

Storage 6 months in airtight container lined with wax paper, in a cool place

INGREDIENTS

2oz	Shelled almonds, with skins	50g
	Groundnut oil	
6oz	Granulated sugar	175g
4fl oz	Water	120ml
	Pinch of cream of tartar	

METHOD

1 Preheat the oven to 425F (220C) Gas 7. Chop almonds and place on baking tray. Put into oven, near top, for a few minutes to brown. Remove and set aside. Lightly oil a baking tray.
2 Put sugar and water into a saucepan and stir over a gentle heat until sugar has dissolved. Gradually bring to the boil and simmer without stirring until

Left: Cherry layer dessert, cherries alternating with thick creamy whip

it is golden brown. Watch care[f]ully because it can rapidly burn.
3 Remove from heat. Stir in crea[m of] tartar and almonds using the w[ell] oiled handle of a wooden spoon. P[our] at once on to oiled baking tray [and] leave to set.
4 Break into small pieces or place [in a] greaseproof bag and crush with rolli[ng] pin.

Cherry meringues

Mini meringues, cherries in a wine-enriched sauce, ice cream and sweetened whipped cream are combined to make a good-looking but simple to prepare dessert that children of all ages appreciate

DESSERT Serves

Overall timing 25 minutes plus coolin[g] time

Equipment Saucepan, measuring jug, 3 bowls, piping bag with large star noz[zle]

Freezing Not recommended

INGREDIENTS

2lb	Can of red cherries	1kg
4oz	Sugar	125g
9fl oz	Cherry juice	250ml
2 tbsp	Dry white wine	2×15m[l]
2 tbsp	Rum	2×15m[l]
3 teasp	Arrowroot	3×5ml
	Red food colouring	
	Vanilla ice cream	
12	Small meringues	12
¼ pint	Carton of double cream	150ml
¼ teasp	Vanilla essence	1.25ml
1 tbsp	Caster sugar	15ml

METHOD

1 Drain cherries. Reserve some for decor[a]tion and put rest in a saucepan wi[th] sugar, cherry juice, wine and rum a[nd] heat gently.
2 Mix arrowroot with a little cold wat[er] and stir into cherry mixture with a fe[w] drops of food colouring. Cook, stirri[ng] till clear, then pour into a bowl. Lea[ve] to cool in fridge.
3 Cut ice cream into 6 slices and pla[ce] on serving dishes. Put a meringue [on] each side of the ice cream, spoon th[e] cherry mixture round the edges.
4 Whip cream, vanilla essence and sug[ar] until stiff. Spoon it into piping bag an[d] using a large star nozzle, pipe crea[m] over the ice cream and meringue[s.] Decorate with reserved cherries an[d] serve immediately.

herry brandy ice

ere are 2 types of cherry brandy —
e spirit and the liqueur; be
re to use the liqueur in this
ipe as the sweetness is needed.
resh cherries are in season,
ne and use instead of glacé ones

SSERT	Serves 6–8

erall timing 10 minutes plus
ceration and chilling

uipment 3 bowls, freezer tray,
ving glasses

ezing Complete Steps 1 and 2, foil-
ap, seal, label and freeze. Freezer life:
nonths. To use: soften in fridge for
minutes before serving

GREDIENTS

	Glacé cherries	12
bsp	Cherry brandy	3×15ml
int	Carton of single cream	150ml
	Block of Italian-style vanilla ice cream	1

ETHOD
1 Chop cherries finely and place in a
bowl with the liqueur. Leave to
macerate for 30 minutes. Whip the
cream to soft peaks.
2 Soften the ice cream in a large bowl
and fold in the cream with the cherries
and liqueur. Pour into freezer tray and
freeze for 2–3 hours until firm.
3 Remove from freezer, divide between
glasses and serve immediately, decorated with crisp fan wafers.

urprise omelette

vo light and fluffy omelettes are
ndwiched together with ice cream
d covered with a jam sauce to
ake a mouthwatering dessert*

SSERT	Serves 6

erall timing 30 minutes

uipment Omelette pan, small
ucepan

ezing Not recommended

INGREDIENTS

6	Eggs	6
6 tbsp	Caster sugar	6×15ml
¼ pint	Milk	150ml
1 teasp	Vanilla essence	5ml
2oz	Butter	50g
6 tbsp	Jam or marmalade	6×15ml
2 tbsp	Lemon juice	2×15ml
	Ice cream	

METHOD
1 To make omelette, separate 3 of the
eggs. Put the yolks in a bowl with the
3 whole eggs and the caster sugar and
beat till light and frothy. Stir in milk
and essence.
2 In another bowl, beat the egg whites
till very stiff. Stir 1 tbsp (15ml) of them
into yolk mixture to lighten it, then
carefully fold in the rest with a metal
spoon.
3 Melt half the butter in an omelette pan.
When it begins to turn a light brown,
pour in half the egg mixture. Cover and
cook over a low heat for 5–7 minutes.
From time to time, lift up edges of
omelette with a wooden spatula to
prevent sticking. When cooked, slide
omelette on to serving dish and keep
it warm. Make a second omelette in
the same way.
4 Put jam or marmalade and lemon juice
in pan and heat through gently.
5 Place one omelette on serving plate
and spread with ice cream. Cover with
second omelette and spoon sauce over.
Cut into wedges to serve.

Stracchino gelato

An excellent way to liven up a
block of bought ice cream is to
serve it with a sauce — here a rich
chocolate one is used. If you like,
choose two complementary flavours
and freeze them in layers

DESSERT	Serves 4–6

Overall timing 20 minutes

Equipment Bowl, saucepan

Freezing Not recommended

INGREDIENTS

	Chocolate sauce (see page 24)	
	Chocolate and vanilla ice cream	
4–6	Sponge fingers	4–6

METHOD
1 Make chocolate sauce according to
instructions on page 24.
2 Turn ice cream out on to chilled serving
plate and press sponge fingers into the
top. Pour some of the chocolate sauce
over. Serve immediately with langue
de chat biscuits and remaining sauce.

ght: Stracchino gelato — two flavours of
cream served with a chocolate sauce

Coupes glacées aux pêches

Using our peach ice cream recipe on page 6, this is a particularly refreshing dessert to serve after a curry or other spicy dish

DESSERT Serves 4

Overall timing 40 minutes plus maceration

Equipment Bowl, saucepan, serving glasses

Freezing Not recommended

INGREDIENTS

4	Large ripe peaches	4
2 tbsp	Maraschino or Peach brandy	2×15ml
3oz	Caster sugar	75g
	Peach ice cream (recipe page 6)	
2 tbsp	Apricot jam	2×15ml

METHOD

1 Peel, halve and stone 2 of the peach Roughly chop the flesh and put i a bowl with the Maraschino and su Macerate in fridge for 30 minu Transfer ice cream to fridge to so for 30 minutes.

2 In a saucepan, melt the apricot j with 1 tbsp (15ml) of macera liquid. Peel, halve and stone remain peaches. Divide all chopped fruit juices between serving dishes and each with cubes of ice cream an peach half. Spoon the warmed j over and serve immediately.

Below: Coupes glacées aux pêches — individual servings topped with fresh peaches

...namon ice cream

... pretty, mushroom-pink coloured
...ream is simple to make and very
...my. Delicious by itself, it also
...plements a spiced fruit salad – add
...amon and cloves to heated juice

...SERT   Serves 4–6

...all timing 45 minutes plus freezing

...pment 3 bowls, saucepan, freezer
...s

...zing Cover and label. Freezer life:
...onths. To use: remove from freezer
...minutes before serving

...REDIENTS

	Eggs	4
	Icing sugar	25g
...sp	Ground cinnamon	15ml
...sp	Clear honey	4×15ml
...nt	Carton of double cream	284ml

...THOD
...eparate the eggs. Put the yolks in a
...owl, sift in the icing sugar and cinna-
...non and blend with a fork till smooth.
...ut the egg whites in another bowl.
...Measure the honey into a saucepan
...nd bring to the boil. Pour at once on
...o the egg yolk mixture, beating con-
...inuously until cool and thickened.
...our the cream into a bowl, whisk
...ightly until thick but still of a pouring
...onsistency. Stir into egg yolk mixture
...nd mix well.
...eat the egg whites until they hold soft
...eaks, then fold into the egg and cream
...mixture. Pour into the freezer trays,
...over and freeze until firm. Remove 45
...minutes before serving to soften. Serve
...vith wafer biscuits or sponge fingers.

...RIATION
...on ice cream into a 1½ pint (850ml)
...uld, cover and freeze. Turn out on to
...ving plate and decorate with glacé
...ts, crystallized violets or whipped
...am, piped over in decorative swirls.

Ways to freeze bananas

Bananas cannot be frozen as whole fruit as this destroys their flavour and texture. They can only be frozen successfully if they are first puréed or used in made-up dishes such as ice cream or fools. Below are two suggestions for ices – one made with yogurt and the other with cream. Make sure you use only firm, just-ripe bananas or they will change colour too quickly. Both dishes can be made well in advance to save you last-minute effort

Banana and orange ice

A healthy, fruity dessert that can be made well in advance. It would be an ideal dish to serve at a dinner party

DESSERT   Serves 6–8

Overall timing 6½ hours including freezing time

Equipment Blender, 2 freezer trays or plastic ice cream carton

Freezing See Method. Freezer life: 2 months. To use: thaw at room temperature for about 15 minutes

INGREDIENTS

1lb	Oranges	450g
1lb	Bananas	450g
3×5oz	Cartons of natural yogurt	3×141g
4 tbsp	Honey	4×15ml

METHOD
1 Squeeze oranges. Peel and chop bananas. Put them both into a blender with the yogurt and honey. Blend till smooth.
2 Place in shallow trays or plastic carton, leaving a little room for expansion, and freeze.
3 After 2 hours, remove from freezer, return ice mixture to blender and blend again for 10 seconds. Pour back into trays or carton, return to freezer and freeze again.
4 Remove trays or carton from freezer when the ice has frozen to a mushy, not solid, state (this takes about 4 hours). Blend once more for 15 seconds then return to the freezer until firm. Serve garnished with slices of fresh banana or with chocolate sauce (see Copacabana bananas, recipe page 31).

Banana ice cream

A refreshing, superbly textured ice cream to refresh the palate after a rich and filling meal

DESSERT   Serves 4–6

Overall timing 1 hour 10 minutes plus freezing time

Equipment Rotary or electric beater, 2 bowls, freezer tray

Freezing Cover and label. Freezer life: 3 months. To use: remove from freezer about 10 minutes before serving

INGREDIENTS

1	Banana	1
6oz	Caster sugar	175g
2 tbsp	Lemon juice	2×15ml
2 tbsp	Orange juice	2×15ml
8fl oz	Milk	220ml
¼ pint	Carton of double cream	150ml

METHOD
1 Set freezer to lowest temperature.
2 Using a rotary or electric beater, mix together peeled, mashed banana and sugar till thick and creamy. Add juices, then milk and continue to mix until smooth. Pour into freezer tray and put in freezer.
3 Meanwhile, whip double cream till stiff and place in fridge.
4 When crystals form at edges of the tray, remove banana mixture from freezer and turn out of the tray into a bowl. Working quickly, beat mixture to a smooth consistency then carefully fold in the cream with a spatula. Return tray to freezer for 1–2 hours.

VARIATION
This banana ice cream can become like a *cassata* by adding 2oz (50g) chopped glacé cherries or candied mixed peel, and 2 tbsp (2×15ml) chopped walnuts to mixture before the cream is folded in.

Coconut ice cream

As this ice cream uses coconut milk – which isn't milk from the nut, but made from the grated flesh – this is a good recipe for getting the best out of the popular prize at carnivals

DESSERT   Serves 8–10

Overall timing 7 hours

Equipment Large saucepan, 2 freezer trays, 2 bowls, rigid container (optional)

Freezing See method. Freezer life: 2 months. To use: thaw in fridge for 1 hour to soften

INGREDIENTS

1 pint	Coconut milk (see Cook's know-how, right)	560ml
4oz	Caster sugar	125g
½ teasp	Vanilla essence	2.5ml
	Pinch of salt	
½ pint	Carton of double cream	284ml

METHOD
1 Preset freezer to lowest temperature 1 hour before freezing.
2 Put coconut milk, sugar, vanilla essence and salt into a pan and stir over a gentle heat till sugar dissolves.
3 Leave to cool. Pour into freezer trays and place in freezer.
4 Meanwhile, whip double cream till soft peaks form, then place in fridge.
5 After 2 hours, crystals should have formed at the edge of the coconut mixture. Remove trays. Turn coconut mixture into a bowl. Working quickly, beat to a smooth consistency, then carefully fold in chilled whipped cream.
6 Divide mixture between freezer trays or rigid container and freeze again for 3 hours. Return freezer setting to normal.
7 Remove from freezer and place in the fridge for 1 hour before serving to soften and develop flavour.

VARIATIONS
To make a chocolate coconut ice cream, break up 4oz (125g) plain dessert chocolate and place in a bowl over hot water to melt. Add it to the coconut milk mixture at Step 2 after the sugar has dissolved, and stir well to combine.
To add banana flavour to this ice cream, mash a peeled banana with 1 tbsp (15ml) lemon juice till creamy, then whisk into the cooled coconut milk mixture.

Apricot ice

A refreshingly different ice from Germany—guests will be surprised to discover that it's not orange!—and several other delicious variations can be made. Cool for a summer day, it is also a good finish for a meal which has included hot and spicy food. The cream and chocolate curl decoration is simple enough to do in a few seconds—before the ice has time to melt

DESSERT   Serves 6

Overall timing 2¾ hours for dried apricots, 35 minutes if using fresh apricots, plus 3 hours freezing

Equipment Bowl, saucepan, coarse sieve or blender, ice-cube trays, 6 individual serving glasses

Freezing Follow Steps 1 to 3, then cover and label, once frozen. Freezer life: 3 months. To use: see Step 4

INGREDIENTS

8oz	Dried apricots *or*	225g
1lb	Fresh apricots	450g
1 pint	Apricot water or water	560ml
8oz	Caster sugar	225g
2 tbsp	Lemon juice	2×15ml

METHOD
1 Cover dried apricots with boiling water and soak for 2 hours. Drain the apricots, saving juice. Or wash the fresh apricots and remove the stones. Bring the apricot water or water to the boil in a saucepan.
2 Add the apricots and sugar and cook for 15 minutes for dried apricots or 5 minutes for fresh. Leave to cool.
3 Purée apricots and syrup by pressing through a coarse sieve or blending in a liquidizer. Add the lemon juice and pour mixture into ice-cube trays. Freeze for 3 hours in the freezing compartment of the fridge or in the freezer.
4 Run ice-cube trays under water for a few seconds, then turn out the frozen cubes. Divide between serving dishes.

TO SERVE
Decorate with a swirl of whipped cream and chocolate curls.

VARIATION
Other fruits can be used in this recipe, for example, strawberries, raspberries, blackcurrants, blackberries, blueberries.

Above: Apricot ice – cool and fruity cube

It's a good way to use surplus fruits season. If using citrus fruits, for examp oranges or mandarins, use ½ pint (300r squeezed fruit juice and 13fl oz (375r water. Stir in 11oz (300g) sugar unti dissolves completely. Place in ice-cu trays and freeze for 4 hours. If usi lemons, use 13fl oz (375ml) juice, ½ pi (300ml) water plus sugar. If freezing i in a container deeper than an ice-cu tray, allow an extra hour's freezing tim

Butterscotch ice cream

Gelatine is used to prevent the formation of large crystals in ice creams, ensuring a soft velvety textu

DESSERT   Serves

Overall timing 25 minutes plus coolin and freezing

Equipment Bowl, 2 saucepans, freezer tray

Freezing See Method. Freezer life: 2 months. To use: remove from freezer 10 minutes before serving

osp	Water	2×15ml
asp	Powdered gelatine	2×5ml
	Unsalted butter	125g
	Soft brown sugar	75g
	Large can of evaporated milk	1

THOD

Put the water in a bowl, sprinkle the gelatine over and leave to sponge. Stand bowl over a pan of simmering water and stir until gelatine dissolves. Remove from heat and leave to cool. Put the butter and sugar in a pan and heat gently until the sugar dissolves. Remove from heat and stir in the evaporated milk.

As soon as the milk and gelatine mixtures are at the same temperature, trickle the gelatine into the milk, whisking well. Pour mixture into freezer tray and freeze until mushy. Remove from freezer and turn mixture into a bowl. Beat thoroughly, then return to freezer tray and freeze till firm.

Above: Blackcurrant sorbet – a refreshing dessert for a warm summer day

Blackcurrant sorbet

The splendid colour of the summer fruit makes this a dramatic dessert to serve – perfect when the weather is hot, and good for refreshing the palate after a highly flavoured main course. If you need to top up the fruit purée, try adding diluted blackcurrant cordial or *cassis* liqueur for even more flavour

DESSERT Serves 8

Overall timing $4\frac{1}{2}$ hours including refrigeration

Equipment $1\frac{1}{2}$ pint (850ml) shallow container, $1\frac{3}{4}$ pint (1 litre) mould

Freezing Freeze in the mould, overwrapped in foil. Freezer life: 1 year. To use: soften for about 20 minutes before serving

INGREDIENTS

2lb	Blackcurrants	900g
9oz	Caster sugar	250g
2	Egg whites	2
	Blackcurrant cordial or liqueur	
	Water	

METHOD

1 Set freezer compartment to maximum. Wash blackcurrants, keep a handful on one side and put the rest through a food mill or sieve to make a purée. Measure the purée – you should have about 1 pint (560ml). Top up with blackcurrant cordial or liqueur and/or water if necessary.

2 Stir the sugar into the purée and mix well to dissolve sugar. Pour into a shallow container and place in the freezer compartment of fridge or in freezer.

3 Leave for about 2 hours until the purée is semi-set. Beat the egg whites till stiff. Remove purée from freezer, mash lightly with a fork, then fold in the whisked egg whites, stirring to distribute evenly through purée.

4 Turn purée into lightly oiled or wetted mould or container. Place in freezer for 2 hours till firmly set.

5 Place mould in hot water up to the rim, then quickly turn sorbet out on to a serving dish. Decorate sorbet with remaining blackcurrants but allow to soften at room temperature for 20 minutes before serving.

cook's know-how

Coconut milk (*santen* in Indonesian) can be made from fresh or desiccated coconut, and is used to flavour many soups, sauces and puddings. To make, grate the flesh of 1 coconut into bowl and add $\frac{1}{4}$ pint (150ml) boiling water. Allow to stand for 20 minutes. Squeeze out handfuls of the flesh so that the water turns white. Continue this squeezing out process for about a minute, making sure that at the end all the liquid has been removed from the flesh. Strain the liquid through a fine sieve. Return grated flesh to the bowl, add more water and repeat process – until you have 1 pint (560ml). To make *santen* from desiccated coconut, put 12oz (350g) coconut and $\frac{1}{4}$ pint (150ml) water into a pan and bring to the boil. Allow to cool, then squeeze out the coconut and continue the process as before, when using fresh coconut.

cook's know-how

You can easily change this sorbet into ice cream by adding whipped double cream to the blackcurrant juice before the second freezing.

Chestnut ice cream

DESSERT   Serves 4

Overall timing 1 hour plus freezing time

Equipment Saucepan, 2 bowls, sieve or blender, 2 pint (1.1 litre) freezer tray or mould

Freezer Make up to Step 3, seal, label and freeze. Freezer life: 2 months. To use: thaw to soften, then decorate

INGREDIENTS

1¼lb	Fresh chestnuts	600g
5oz	Caster sugar	150g
2 tbsp	Rum	2×15ml
½ teasp	Vanilla essence	2.5ml
½ pint	Carton of double cream	284ml
	Decoration (optional)	
¼ pint	Carton of double or whipping cream	150ml
	Crystallized violets	

Below: Chestnut ice cream – serve as a block or in individual scoops

METHOD

1 Put the prepared chestnuts in a pan of boiling water and cook for 10 minutes, then peel and skin. Return chestnuts to the pan, cover again with water and simmer gently for 15–20 minutes or until tender.

2 Drain chestnuts and press through a sieve or purée in a blender. Put purée in a large bowl and mix in the sugar, rum and vanilla essence.

3 In another bowl, lightly whip the cream until just stiff, then fold into purée. Place in freezer tray or mould and freeze for about 1½ hours or until just setting. Take out, mash well with a fork to break up ice crystals and return to freezer. Repeat mashing process after 1½ hours.

4 For a decorated dessert in a tray, whip remaining cream until stiff. Using a piping bag with a rose or star nozzle, pipe border of cream around ice cream in freezer tray. If ice cream is in a mould, dip it quickly in and out of bowl of hot water, invert over serving dish. Or thaw till just soft and serve individual scoops of ice cream. Decorate with piped rosettes of whipped cream and a few crystallized violets or pieces of finely chopped preserved ginger if liked.

Time-saver ice cream

An easy to make ice cream dessert that uses storecupboard ingredient Two different ice creams — one honey, the other flavoured with glacé fruits and lemon rind — are frozen till mushy, then layered in a mould and frozen till firm

DESSERT   Serves

Overall timing 25 minutes plus freezi

Equipment 3 bowls, 2 freezer trays, 2½ pint (1.5 litre) bombe mould or pudding basin

Freezing Freeze in mould, cover. Free life: 2 months. To use: soften in fridg for 30 minutes before serving

INGREDIENTS

¾ pint	Double cream	400m
3 tbsp	Runny honey	3×15
¼ teasp	Vanilla essence	1.25m
15oz	Can of ready-made custard	425g
1	Packet of instant dessert topping	1
¼ pint	Cold milk	150ml
3oz	Glacé fruits	75g
	Grated rind of 1 lemon	

METHOD

1 Chill mould in freezer. Whip the cre till soft peaks form. Remove a third the cream, put into another bowl a reserve. Whisk the honey, van essence and canned custard into first lot of cream. Put into freezer tr and freeze till mushy.

2 Whisk the dessert topping and m together until thick and foamy. Fold the reserved cream, chopped glacé fru and grated lemon rind. Put into free tray and freeze till mushy.

3 Remove first ice cream from the free and spoon into the mould, pressing against the sides in a thick layer a leaving a space in the middle.

4 Remove second ice cream from free and spoon into centre of mould, pre ing down well. Smooth surface, cov and return to freezer until firm.

TO SERVE

Place mould in fridge for 30 minut before serving to allow ice cream to softe Dip mould in hot water up to the rim, the turn out on to chilled serving plate a serve immediately.

ranité de café

refreshing water ice, a granité
based on a thin sugar syrup
which a flavouring – in this
e coffee – is added. Don't be
pted to stir the mixture
ile it is freezing as this will
vent granules from forming

SSERT   Serves 6–8

erall timing 2 hours

uipment Saucepan, fine sieve or
slin-lined sieve, freezer tray, bowl

ezing Cover, label and refreeze.
ezer life: 6 months. To use: thaw
soft enough to fork into glasses

GREDIENTS

	Granulated sugar	250g
bsp	Vanilla sugar	15ml
int	Water	560ml
easp	Instant coffee granules	8×5ml
int	Carton of whipping cream	300ml
	Peppermint essence	

METHOD

1 Put granulated and *vanilla sugar and water in a saucepan over moderate heat. Stir until sugar is completely dissolved, then bring to the boil and boil hard for 5 minutes. Skim if necessary.
2 Stir in the coffee granules and remove pan from heat. Allow mixture to cool completely.
3 Pour coffee mixture through a fine sieve or muslin-lined sieve into a freezer tray. Place in freezer or freezing compartment of fridge and leave for about 1 hour or until the mixture forms a granular mass. Do not stir.
4 In a bowl whisk cream till just holding soft peaks, then add a few drops of peppermint essence, if using, to taste.
5 Scrape out contents of freezer tray with a fork and divide ice between chilled serving glasses. Top each glass with peppermint-flavoured cream and serve with Breton biscuits or wafers.

*Although packets of vanilla sugar can be bought, it can easily be made at home. Place 1–2 split vanilla pods in an airtight container with sugar, seal and leave for 1–2 weeks until vanilla flavour has been absorbed by the sugar. Take out pods and store in airtight container for further use.

ow: Granité de café – crunchy coffee ice topped with peppermint cream

MILKY ICE POPS

These lollies are made from milk, sugar and condensed milk – try them instead of fruit ones for a change. They keep well in the freezer.
Place ¾ pint (400ml) milk in a saucepan. Blend 2 teasp (2×5ml) custard powder with 2 tbsp (2×15ml) caster sugar and a little water and stir into milk. Bring to the boil and cook for 3 minutes, stirring. Remove from heat and plunge bottom of pan into cold water to cool quickly. Stir in ½ a can of condensed milk, 1 teasp (5ml) vanilla essence and another ½ pint (300ml) milk. Mix till well combined, then pour into ice lolly moulds or ice cube trays and put in the freezer. When half frozen, push wooden sticks in if using moulds to make ice lollies. Then leave till mixture is hard. Freezer life: 2 months.

Grapefruit and peppermint sorbet

A refreshingly light and tangy ice flavoured with mint liqueur

DESSERT   Serves 4

Overall timing 20 minutes plus freezing

Equipment Saucepan, rigid container, bowl

Freezing See Method

INGREDIENTS

4oz	Caster sugar	125g
¼ pint	Water	150ml
½ pint	Grapefruit juice	300ml
3 tbsp	Crème de menthe	3×15ml
2	Egg whites	2

METHOD

1 Put the sugar and water into a pan, bring to the boil and cook for 5 minutes. Remove from heat and stir in grapefruit juice and Crème de menthe. Cool.
2 Turn mixture into rigid container and freeze till mushy.
3 Whisk egg whites in a bowl till stiff but not dry. Remove mixture from freezer, mash to break up the crystals, then carefully fold in the whisked whites. Return to freezer till firm.

Creamy iced melon

A dessert to make when melons are abundant. The ice cream itself is refreshing and delicious and other fruits can be added to vary the flavour and texture. A treat to produce from the freezer when memories of summer are fading

DESSERT   Serves 4–6

Overall timing 20 minutes plus chilling

Equipment Blender, bowl, freezer tray

Freezing Freeze in tray, cover and label. Freezer life: 2 months. To use: transfer to fridge to soften 30 minutes before serving

INGREDIENTS

1	Large ripe honeydew melon	1
3oz	Caster sugar	75g
½ pint	Carton of double cream	284ml

METHOD
1 Slice the top off the melon, remove and discard the seeds. Scoop out flesh and place in blender. Chill the shell.
2 Add sugar to melon flesh and blend till smooth. Whip the cream to soft peaks in a large bowl. Fold in the purée and pour into a freezer tray.
3 Freeze for about 2 hours till mushy. Turn into a bowl and beat well. Return to freezer tray and freeze till firm.

TO SERVE
Place ice cream in fridge for 30 minutes to soften before placing scoops of it in the shell. Serve immediately.

Iced melon and cherry wedges

This attractive melon dessert has a coloured layered effect when the stuffed melon halves are cut into wedges. Serve iced melon plain, or with pouring cream to pass round

DESSERT   Serves 4

Overall timing 25 minutes plus chilling

Equipment Saucepan, melon baller, bowl

Freezing Not recommended

INGREDIENTS

12oz	Ripe cherries	350g
4oz	Caster sugar	125g
1	Green-skinned honeydew melon	1
1 pint	Vanilla ice cream	560ml

METHOD
1 Wash and stone the cherries. Put into a saucepan with the sugar and heat gently, stirring till sugar dissolves. Simmer for 10 minutes, then allow to cool.
2 Slice the melon in half lengthways. Remove and discard the seeds. Scoop out flesh with a melon baller, add to the cherries and mix well. Chill the fruit and melon shells for at least 2 hours.
3 Pack each melon half tightly with alternate strips of ice cream and the fruit mixture. Cover and place in freezer for 1 hour.

TO SERVE
Cut each half in half across the strips so that each serving has equal portions of fruit and ice cream.

Above: Chocolate ice cream – rich and thick and very simple to make

Chocolate ice crear

This ice cream is delicious with cream or as part of a composite dis

DESSERT   Serves

Overall timing 4 hours including freezing time

Equipment 2 bowls, saucepan, freezer container, piping bag, serving glasses

Freezing See method. Freezer life: 2 months

INGREDIENTS

1 pint	Milk	560m
3oz	Sugar	75g
	Pinch of salt	
4oz	Bitter chocolate	125g
4	Egg yolks	4
	Decoration	
¼ pint	Carton of whipping or double cream	150ml
2 teasp	Icing sugar	2×5m
6	Maraschino cherries	6
2 teasp	Chocolate vermicelli	2×5m

Chocolate sauce

A sauce to be eaten hot rather than cold. It is especially good over ice cream with a sprinkling of nuts, or fresh or grilled bananas

HOT DESSERT SAUCE   Makes ½ pint (300ml)

Overall timing 15 minutes

Equipment Bowl, saucepan

Freezing Cool, then pour into rigid container. Cover, label and freeze. Freezer life: 1 month. To use: thaw for 1 hour, then heat gently

INGREDIENTS

2 teasp	Cornflour	2×5ml
½ pint	Cold milk	300ml
2oz	Plain dessert chocolate	50g
2 tbsp	Granulated sugar	2×15ml
½ teasp	Vanilla essence	2.5ml

METHOD
1 Blend the cornflour in a bowl with a little milk. Put rest of milk in saucepan with the broken up chocolate. Heat slowly until the chocolate melts, then stir in cornflour.
2 Cook, stirring constantly, until the sauce comes to the boil and thickens. Stir in sugar and essence and cook, stirring, for 3 minutes more. Serve.

elt chocolate, milk, sugar and salt
saucepan and stir until dissolved

ld chocolate mixture to warmed, beaten
g yolks, mix till creamy, then cool

ETHOD

Set freezer to fast freeze.

Heat milk, sugar and salt in a saucepan. Break chocolate into milk and stir well till dissolved. Remove from heat.

Beat egg yolks in a bowl. Place bowl over a pan of boiling water. Stir in the chocolate mixture from the other bowl. Mix for 5–8 minutes till creamy, then remove from heat and stand the bowl in cold water.

When cool, transfer to a freezer container, cover and place in freezing compartment of fridge or freezer for 45 minutes. Remove mixture from fridge and stir to keep ice crystals small. Repeat after 30 minutes, and again after next 30 minutes. Leave for further 2 hours.

Beat cream with icing sugar in a bowl till stiff. Spoon into a piping bag with a star nozzle and place in fridge.

Place ice cream in ordinary part of fridge 45 minutes before serving. Cut into pieces and divide between the serving glasses. Pipe cream over, sprinkle with chocolate vermicelli and put a cherry on top of each. Or slice and place inside meringue case.

Angel pie

A frothy concoction which combines meringue, chocolate ice cream and a chocolate and cream topping. The egg yolks are used to make the ice cream and the egg whites to make the meringue (colour it with cocoa if you prefer) – and it's all as simple as pie

DESSERT Serves 6

Overall timing 20 minutes plus 1 hour chilling time

Equipment Mixing bowl, electric or rotary mixer

Freezing Not recommended

Below: Angel pie – combining the best of popular desserts, chocolate, meringue, ice cream and cream

INGREDIENTS

½ pint	Carton of double cream	284ml
4oz	Plain or bitter chocolate	125g
2 tbsp	Icing sugar	2×15ml
1	Large meringue case	1
	Chocolate ice cream (opposite)	

METHOD

1 About an hour in advance, put the cream in a mixing bowl in the fridge.
2 Coarsely grate the chocolate and keep any leftover pieces for decoration.
3 Remove cream from fridge. It should have the consistency of custard. If it is too thick, add a few drops of cold water. Beat with mixer until it begins to stick to the beaters and is stiff.
4 Gradually stir in the icing sugar. Fill the meringue case with chocolate ice cream, then spoon the whipped cream over it. Sprinkle generously with the grated chocolate. Serve immediately. Eat the same day.

25

Pineapple gondolas

The shell of a pineapple provides two cases to hold fruit and ice cream – splendid party centrepiece

DESSERT   Serves 6

Overall timing 25 minutes plus chilling

Equipment Grapefruit knife, 2 bowls, piping bag with large star nozzle

Freezing Not recommended

INGREDIENTS

1	Large ripe pineapple	1
3 tbsp	Icing sugar	3×15ml
2 tbsp	Rum	2×15ml
2	Bananas	2
2 tbsp	Lemon juice	2×15ml
1lb	Strawberries	450g
¼ pint	Carton of double cream	150ml
1	Block of vanilla ice cream	1

METHOD

1 Cut the pineapple in half lengthways, cutting through the leaves as well. Scoop flesh out with a grapefruit knife, discarding hard core. Chop flesh, put into a bowl with the sifted icing sugar and rum and chill for 30 minutes.
2 Peel and slice bananas. Toss in lemon juice and mix into pineapple mixture. Wash and hull strawberries.
3 Arrange pineapple shells on serving platter. Just before serving, spoon ice cream into bottom of shells, then top with pineapple and banana mixture.
4 Whip cream in a bowl till stiff, then spoon into piping bag fitted with large star nozzle.
5 Pipe cream round the top edges of the pineapple shells, decorate with strawberries and serve immediately.

To make Crème Chantilly to serve with desserts, put ½ pint (284ml) double cream, 1 tbsp (15ml) cold milk and an ice cube in a bowl. Beat slowly, incorporating as much air into cream as you can. When cream thickens add 1 tbsp (15ml) caster sugar and beat till mixture holds soft peaks and is light.

Above: Iced grape dessert – the deep, rich colour comes from black grapes, the flavour from syrup, wine and lemon juice

Iced grape dessert

A dessert with a most attractive colour and good texture. Try it for a special occasion or to finish a particularly rich or spicy meal. Make up a batch for the freezer when grapes are not so expensive

DESSERT   Serves 4

Overall timing 20 minutes plus freezing

Equipment Saucepan, sieve, bowl, freezer tray

Freezing See Method. Freezer life: 3–6 months. To use: serve straight from freezer

INGREDIENTS

1¼lb	Black grapes	600g
1 tbsp	Lemon juice	15ml
3fl oz	Dry white wine	90ml
1 tbsp	Maraschino	15ml
4oz	Cane or golden syrup	125g

METHOD

1 Wash grapes and remove from ste[m] Put into a pan with the lemon juic[e] wine and Maraschino. Bring to t[he] boil, then simmer gently for 5 minut[es] or until soft.
2 Remove from heat and press throu[gh] a sieve into a bowl. Allow to co[ol] slightly, then stir in the syrup.
3 Turn mixture into freezer tray. Lea[ve] to cool completely, then place [in] freezer and freeze until firm. Scoop in[to] individual glasses and serve with cri[sp] almond biscuits.

:e cream layer cake

rich, frozen "cake" for a special
:asion such as a child's party.
ree flavours of ice cream are
zen in layers in a tin, then
mpletely covered with cream and
oped with chocolate and cherries

:SSERT Cuts into 8

erall timing 1½ hours

uipment 8 inch (20cm) round cake
, bowl, piping bag and star nozzle

ezing Makes as Steps 1–4. Cover,
el and freeze. Freezer life: 2 months.
use: soften in fridge for 15–20
nutes, then complete Steps 5–7

GREDIENTS

int	Praline ice cream	560ml
int	Peach ice cream	560ml
int	Coffee ice cream	560ml
int	Carton of double cream	284ml
z	Plain dessert chocolate	50g
	Maraschino cherries	8

:THOD

Remove praline ice cream from freezer
and leave to soften in the fridge for
15–20 minutes.
Spoon praline ice cream over the base
of the cake tin and smooth surface.
Return to freezer for 20 minutes.
Meanwhile, remove peach ice cream
from freezer and soften in fridge.
Remove cake tin from freezer, spread
softened peach ice cream on top and
smooth surface. Return to freezer for
20 minutes. Meanwhile, remove coffee
ice cream from freezer and soften in
fridge.
Take cake tin out of freezer and spread
coffee ice cream on top. Smooth surface
and return to freezer until all the layers
are firm.
Whip the cream until stiff. Grate the
chocolate. Remove cake tin from freezer
and dip into hot water for 5–10 seconds
to loosen ice cream. Turn out on to
chilled serving plate.
Spread two-thirds of the whipped
cream over the base and sides of the
cake. Press grated chocolate around
the sides of the cake and mark the top
into 8 slices.
Spoon remaining cream into piping
bag fitted with star nozzle. Pipe swirls
on to marked slices and decorate with
cherries. Place in fridge for 30 minutes
before serving.

Glace flambée aux framboises

A flambé is always a spectacular way to end a meal, and here the
contrast between the warm Kirsch or brandy and the cold vanilla ice
cream is particularly effective. Raspberries add the finishing touch

DESSERT Serves 6

Overall timing 10 minutes plus 2 hours
maceration

Equipment Bowl, saucepan, metal ladle

Freezing Not recommended

INGREDIENTS

12oz	Fresh or frozen raspberries	350g
2–4oz	Caster sugar	50–125g
3 tbsp	Lemon juice	3×15ml
1½ pints	Vanilla ice cream	850ml
3 tbsp	Kirsch or brandy	3×15ml

METHOD

1 Put raspberries, sugar (add according
to taste) and lemon juice in a bowl and
macerate for 2 hours in the fridge. Chill
serving plate.
2 Transfer raspberries and soaking juices
to pan and heat through gently.
3 Remove ice cream from freezer and
place on serving plate. Spoon raspberries and syrup over. Warm Kirsch
or brandy in ladle. Set alight and pour
over ice cream. Serve immediately.

Below: Glace flambée aux framboises — a delectable mix of colours and flavours

Above: Mandarines à la niçoise — scoops of mandarine ice cream in shells full of fruit

Mandarines à la niçoise

Shape and texture are important in all *niçoise* dishes. In this luscious dessert, the flesh of the fruits contrasts well with the mandarine ice cream

DESSERT   Serves 8

Overall timing 15 minutes plus 2 hours maceration

Equipment Bowl

Freezing Not recommended

INGREDIENTS

8	Large mandarines	8
1	Peach	1
4oz	Cherries	125g
8oz	Can of pineapple rings	227g
2oz	Caster sugar	50g
2 tbsp	Cointreau	2×15ml
	Mandarine ice cream (recipe right)	

METHOD

1 Wash and dry the mandarines. Slice off the top of each with a sharp knife and reserve. Scoop out the flesh with a teaspoon, taking care not to break the peel. Cover the empty shells and the tops and place in the fridge.
2 Cut the flesh into neat pieces discarding the pips and pith. Peel the peach, cut in half and discard the stone. Cut into cubes. Wash and stone the cherries, then chop flesh. Drain the pineapple and cut into pieces.
3 Put all the fruit into a bowl with the sugar and liqueur and leave for 2 hours to macerate.

4 Remove mandarine shells and tops from the fridge. Divide the fruit and juices between them, add a scoop of ice cream and place the lids on top. Serve immediately in individual glass dishes.

Mandarine ice cream

Ice cream made with puréed mandarine flesh and a little chopped peel. Choose firm fruit so you can serve or freeze the ice in the shells

DESSERT   Serves 6

Overall timing 40 minutes plus freezing

Equipment Blender, 3 bowls, 2 saucepans, sieve, muslin, freezer tray

Freezing Freeze in mandarine shells. Freezer life: 2 months. To use: soften in fridge for 30 minutes before serving

INGREDIENTS

7	Mandarines	7
2	Egg yolks	2
2oz	Caster sugar	50g
½ pint	Milk	300ml
1 teasp	Vanilla essence	5ml
¼ pint	Carton of double cream	150ml

METHOD

1 Wash the mandarines. Cut off tops a scoop out flesh from 6 of them and pla in a blender. Finely chop peel of maining mandarine and add with t flesh to the blender. Purée. Cover emp mandarine shells and place in frid;
2 Put the egg yolks and sugar in a lar bowl and beat till creamy.
3 Put milk and vanilla essence into a p and bring to just under boiling poi Remove from heat.
4 Pour milk in a thin stream on creamed mixture, stirring continuous Place bowl over a pan of simmeri water and cook for about 10 minut without boiling, stirring constantly mixture will coat the back of the spoc
5 Remove from heat and strain throug muslin-lined sieve into a bowl. Pla bowl in larger dish of cold water a beat until cool to prevent skin formin
6 Whisk the cream till it just holds shape, then fold with mandarine pur into cold custard. Pour into freezer tr and freeze for 1½ hours till mushy.
7 Turn ice cream into a bowl and be well. Pour back into container a return to freezer. Freeze till mush
8 Repeat beating process, then spoc into chilled mandarine shells ar return to freezer.* Freeze till firm. Tran fer to fridge 20 minutes before servin

*To frost shells, brush with water firs Lift shells with spoons so there'll be fingerprints in the frost!

oires Hélène

ghtly poached pears served with
e cream and hot chocolate sauce

ESSERT   Serves 6

verall timing 40 minutes plus chilling

quipment 2 saucepans, bowl, ice cream
oop

eezing Not recommended

INGREDIENTS

	Firm pears	6
pint	Water	400ml
tbsp	Lemon juice	15ml
oz	Caster sugar	125g
	Vanilla pod	1
oz	Plain dessert chocolate	100g
oz	Butter	15g
	Vanilla ice cream	
	Crystallized violets	

METHOD

1 Peel the pears and remove the stalks.
  Put the water, lemon juice, sugar and
  vanilla pod into a saucepan and heat
  gently till the sugar dissolves.
2 Bring the syrup to the boil, add the
  peeled pears and simmer for about 15
  minutes till just tender. Leave pears to
  cool in the syrup, then lift them out
  with a draining spoon and chill for
  several hours. Reserve the syrup.
3 Break the chocolate into small pieces
  and put into a bowl with the butter.
  Stand the bowl over a pan of simmering
  water and stir till melted. Remove from
  the heat and beat in 2 tbsp (2×15ml)
  of the pear syrup.
4 Arrange the pears in a serving dish and
  place scoops of ice cream between them.
  Decorate with crystallized violets.
5 Spoon the chocolate sauce over the
  pears and serve immediately.

*Below: Poires Hélène – to stop ice cream
melting too fast, chill serving dish and
scoop, then serve as fast as you can*

Above: Apricot parfait, a creamy dessert

Apricot parfait

An ice cream dessert made with curd
cheese, two fruits and cherry liqueur

DESSERT   Serves 6

Overall timing 10 minutes

Equipment Sieve or liquidizer, 6 glass
serving dishes

Freezing Not recommended

INGREDIENTS

1lb 13oz	Can of apricots	822g
17fl oz	Block of vanilla ice cream	460ml
2oz	Ground almonds	50g
2 tbsp	Maraschino or Kirsch	2×15ml
8oz	Curd cheese	225g
8oz	Raspberries	225g
1 tbsp	Nibbed almonds	15ml

METHOD

1 Drain apricots. Reserve 4 for decoration.
  Press rest through a sieve or liquidize.
2 Quickly mix together the apricot purée,
  ice cream, ground almonds, liqueur
  and curd cheese.
3 Wash and drain raspberries. Divide
  between 6 serving dishes and top with
  apricot cream mixture. Decorate with
  reserved apricots, sliced, and nibbed
  almonds. Serve immediately.

29

Pawpaw sorbet

A refreshing frozen dessert with a definitely tropical taste. Set fridge thermostat to low before starting

DESSERT   Serves 4

Overall timing 20 minutes plus freezing

Equipment Blender, 2 bowls, ice-cube tray

Freezing Freeze in tray, place in plastic bag, seal and label. Freezer life: 6 months. To use: serve from frozen

INGREDIENTS

2	Ripe pawpaws	2
2	Bananas	2
	Juice of 2 limes or 1 large lemon	
5oz	Caster sugar	150g
2	Egg whites	2

METHOD

1 Wash the pawpaws and cut in half lengthways. Remove seeds and skin. Roughly chop the flesh. Peel and chop the bananas and put into a blender with the pawpaw flesh.

Above: Copacabana bananas – a dessert with the Carmen Miranda touch

Left: Pawpaw sorbet – the juice of limes or lemon introduces a tanginess to the combined flavours of pawpaw and banana

2 Add the juice from the limes or lemon to the blender with the sugar. Blend a fairly smooth purée and pour into large bowl.
3 Whisk the egg whites till stiff but n dry, and fold into the purée. Pour in an ice-cube tray, leaving the cube div ders in it, and freeze till firm.
4 Remove the cubes from the tray an serve in chilled tall glasses with cris biscuits and long spoons.

METHOD

1 To make syrup, put the water and sugar into a saucepan. Stir until sugar has dissolved then cook over gentle heat till the syrup starts to thicken.
2 Peel and slice the bananas and add to the saucepan. Cook for 5–7 minutes. Remove from heat, stir in the rum and leave to cool.
3 Meanwhile, make the sauce. Break up the chocolate and put into a bowl with the golden syrup and milk. Place bowl over a pan of hot water and stir over a gentle heat until mixture has melted. Remove from heat, leave to cool slightly.
4 Divide the ice cream among 6 individual serving dishes. Cover with the bananas and top with the warm chocolate sauce. Decorate with fan wafers.

VARIATION

Change the taste by using a different flavoured ice cream. Pistachio would be ideal, or vanilla made crunchy with praline – see recipe page 16.

Mandarine sherbet

Whole mandarines, peel included, are blended and used to make a fluffy and refreshing iced dessert

DESSERT Serves 6

Overall timing 20 minutes plus freezing

Equipment Blender, saucepan, 2 pint (1.1 litre) freezer tray, 2 bowls

Freezing Freeze in tray. Freezer life: 6 months. To use: serve from frozen

INGREDIENTS

4	Large mandarines	4
8oz	Caster sugar	225g
1 pint	Water	560ml
1	Egg white	1

METHOD

1 Wash the mandarines, remove peel and chop. Place in the blender with the flesh and blend to a pulp.
2 Put the sugar and water into a saucepan and heat slowly, stirring until the sugar dissolves. Bring to the boil and simmer for 10 minutes without stirring – do not let it colour. Remove from heat and leave to cool.
3 Stir the mandarine pulp into the syrup, pour into freezer tray and freeze for about 2 hours until mushy.
4 Put the half-frozen mixture into a bowl and beat well. Whisk the egg white in

another bowl till soft peaks form, then fold into beaten mixture. Return mixture to freezer tray and freeze till firm.
5 Spoon into small glasses and serve with crisp biscuits or wafers.

Elderflower sorbet

An old English recipe that takes advantage of the flowers of the wild elder. A head consists of a flat, compact group of flowers at the top of a stem – catch them quickly before the berries form

DESSERT Serves 4

Overall timing 15 minutes plus cooling and freezing

Equipment Saucepan, shallow freezer trays, 2 bowls

Freezing See Method. Freezer life: 3 months. To use: thaw for about 10 minutes at room temperature

INGREDIENTS

1	Lemon	1
4	Heads of elderflower	4
6oz	Caster sugar	175g
1 pint	Water	560ml
1	Egg white	1

METHOD

1 Thinly pare rind from lemon and squeeze out juice. Wash and drain elderflowers.
2 Put sugar and water in a pan and heat, stirring, until sugar dissolves. Add lemon rind and elderflowers, bring to the boil and cook rapidly for 6 minutes. Remove from heat and leave to cool.
3 Stir lemon juice into pan. Strain into ice-cube trays and put in freezer or freezing compartment of fridge until crystals begin to form.
4 Whisk egg white in a bowl till stiff. Turn half-frozen mixture into a bowl, mush with a fork, then fold in whisked whites. Return to ice-cube trays and freeze till firm.

Copacabana bananas

From the USA, this luscious dessert makes an impressive ending to a meal

DESSERT Serves 6

Overall timing 30 minutes

Equipment 2 saucepans, small bowl, individual serving dishes

Freezing Not recommended

INGREDIENTS

pint	Water	150ml
oz	Caster sugar	75g
	Bananas	6
tbsp	Rum	4×15ml
	Sauce	
oz	Plain chocolate	225g
tbsp	Golden syrup	2×15ml
tbsp	Milk	4×15ml
	Block of vanilla ice cream	1
	Fan wafers	6

Maple-walnut ice

Home-made ice cream is always a welcome change. This one can be smooth if you grind the walnuts, or crunchy-textured if you leave them in pieces. Either way it's exquisite

DESSERT   Makes 1 pint (560m

Overall timing 40 minutes plus freezir

Equipment 3 bowls, 2 saucepans, 1 p (560ml) freezer tray

Freezing Freeze in tray or mould, cove and label. Freezer life: 2 months. To use: transfer to the fridge for 30 minutes before serving

INGREDIENTS

2	Egg yolks	2
1 teasp	Vanilla essence	5ml
6 tbsp	Maple syrup	6×15n
½ pint	Milk	300ml
¼ pint	Carton of double cream	150ml
2oz	Walnut pieces	50g

METHOD

1 Put the egg yolks, vanilla and map syrup in a large bowl and beat with wooden spoon till well blended.
2 Pour the milk into a saucepan a bring almost to the boil. Gradually po on to the yolk mixture, stirring co stantly. Place the bowl over a pan simmering water and cook, stirring, f 10 minutes till thick enough to coat th back of the spoon.
3 Remove from the heat and strain in a large bowl. Stand the bowl in c water and stir to prevent a skin formir as it cools.
4 Whip the cream till it just holds shape and fold into the custard. Po into a freezer tray and freeze for abo 1½ hours till mushy. Heat the grill.
5 Meanwhile, finely chop the walnuts an toast under grill till crisp. Allow to coo
6 Empty the half-frozen ice cream into bowl and beat to break down large io crystals. Add the walnuts and mix wel Return to the freezer tray and freez till firm.
7 Transfer to the fridge 30 minutes befor serving with fresh or canned fruit o hot apple pie.

VARIATIONS

For a different banana split, serve scoop of maple-walnut ice on bananas, halve lengthways, with whipped or pourin cream, and top with halved strawberries Or use praline instead of walnuts.

Above: Glace aux myrtilles — French treatment for their favourite berries

Glace aux myrtilles

This gorgeous looking rich sauce for ice cream is very simply made from bilberry jam and Kirsch. Top ices with fan wafers or serve them with almond tuiles (the recipe is on page 41) which can be rolled round the handle of a wooden spoon

DESSERT   Serves 6

Overall timing 15 minutes

Equipment 6 glasses, saucepan

Freezing Not recommended

INGREDIENTS

12oz	Jar of bilberry jam	340g
2 tbsp	Kirsch	2×15ml
1½ pints	Vanilla ice cream	850ml
6	Fan wafers	6

METHOD

1 Put glasses in fridge to chill.
2 Place bilberry jam and Kirsch into a saucepan and beat with a fork over gentle heat till well combined. Leave to cool.
3 Cut ice cream into cubes and divide between chilled glasses. Pour 3 tbsp (3×15ml) of the jam and Kirsch mixture over each. Decorate with fan wafers and serve immediately.

Crêpes Irene

A stylish dessert that can be made from freezer and cupboard

HOT DESSERT   Makes 12

Overall timing 30 minutes

Equipment 2 bowls, measuring jug, 8 inch (20cm) omelette or frying pan, small saucepan

Freezing Make the crêpes but don't fill. Stack with greaseproof paper in between. Wrap in foil, label and freeze. Freezer life: 4 months. To use: unwrap, spread out crêpes and thaw for 30 minutes. Heat in lightly greased pan

INGREDIENTS

	Crêpes	
	Eggs	3
	Pinch of salt	
9 oz	Milk	250ml
2 tbsp	Caster sugar	2×15ml
4 oz	Plain flour	125g
2 oz	Butter	50g
	Topping	
12oz	Can of blackberries	340g
8 tbsp	Honey	8×15ml
4 tbsp	Cognac	4×15ml
1 pint	Vanilla ice cream	500ml
4 oz	Chopped walnuts	125g

Above: Crêpes Irene – a sweet and clever combination, and so easily prepared

METHOD

1 To make crêpes, mix together the eggs, salt, milk and sugar in a bowl. Sift flour into another bowl, making a well in the centre. Pour in liquid and beat or whisk till smooth (this step can be completed in a blender). Pour into jug and leave to stand for 5 minutes.

2 Chop butter into 12 equal pieces. Heat pan, add butter piece and when melted (hot, but not brown) add a twelfth of the batter to make a very thin crêpe. Continue until all crêpes are made. As they are cooked, fold them into quarters, arrange on serving plates and keep warm.

3 Place drained blackberries in a sieve and rinse under running water. Turn on to kitchen paper to drain.

4 In a saucepan, gently heat honey with Cognac. Remove from heat before it boils.

5 To assemble crêpes, put a cube of ice cream on top of each crêpe and scatter with blackberries. Pour over hot honey mixture and sprinkle with chopped walnuts. Serve immediately.

Coupes impératrice

A dessert fit for an empress – a lavish mixture of whipped cream, ice cream and fruit

DESSERT   Serves 4

Overall timing 15 minutes

Equipment 2 bowls, 4 serving glasses

Freezing Not recommended

INGREDIENTS

2oz	Bitter chocolate	50g
1 pint	Vanilla ice cream	560ml
½ pint	Carton of double cream	284ml
2 teasp	Caster sugar	2×5ml
2 tbsp	Maraschino	2×15ml
6oz	Marrons glacés pieces	175g
	Crystallized violets	

METHOD

1 Coarsely grate chocolate. Remove ice cream from fridge and leave to soften slightly. Whisk cream and caster sugar in a bowl till stiff.

2 Quickly mix together chocolate, ice cream, Maraschino and marrons glacés pieces. Divide mixture between serving dishes. Spoon whipped cream on top and decorate with crystallized violets.

Sorbetto alla Marsala

Creamy Marsala ice to serve with crisp finger biscuits or fan wafers

DESSERT — Serves 6

Overall timing 30 minutes plus chilling

Equipment Saucepan, freezer tray, 2 bowls

Freezing See Method. Freezer life: 2 months. To use: thaw at room temperature for 10 minutes

INGREDIENTS

8oz	Caster sugar	225g
1 pint	Water	560ml
2 tbsp	Orange juice	2×15ml
1 tbsp	Lemon juice	15ml
¼ pint	Superiore Marsala	150ml
¼ pint	Carton of double cream	150ml

METHOD

1 Put the sugar and water into a saucepan and heat gently, stirring, till sugar dissolves. Bring to the boil and simmer for 10 minutes without stirring. Do not allow to colour. Remove from the heat and leave to cool.

2 Strain the orange and lemon juice into the syrup. Add all but 4 tbsp (4×15ml) of the Marsala. Mix well and pour into a freezer tray and freeze till mushy.

3 Whip the cream till soft peaks form. Fold in the remaining Marsala. Tip the mushy sorbet into a bowl and carefully fold in the cream with a metal spoon. Return to freezer tray and freeze till firm.

4 Thaw at room temperature for 10 minutes and divide between wine glasses. Serve immediately.

Timbale aux framboises

Roughly crushed meringue shells gi this rich ice cream its unusually crunchy texture. The timbale is generously decorated with fresh frui and accompanied by a thick sauce ma from raspberries, Cointreau and sug

DESSERT — Serves

Overall timing 45 minutes plus freezin and chilling

Equipment 2 bowls, 6 inch (15cm) charlotte mould or loose-bottom cake tin, saucepan

Freezing Freeze timbale in mould or ti cover and label. To freeze sauce, cool, pour into a rigid container, leaving ½ inch (12.5mm) headspace, cover, lab and freeze. Freezer life: 2 months. To use: turn timbale out on to serving dis and leave in fridge for 30 minutes to soften. Thaw sauce at room temperatu for 2–3 hours

INGREDIENTS

¾ pint	Double cream	400ml
4oz	Icing sugar	125g
1 teasp	Vanilla essence	5ml
	Red food colouring	
4oz	Meringue shells	125g
1lb	Raspberries	450g
2 tbsp	Caster sugar	2×15m
3 tbsp	Cointreau	3×15m

METHOD

1 Put the cream, sifted icing sugar an vanilla essence in a bowl with a fe drops of red food colouring and whis till soft peaks form. Roughly crush th meringue shells and fold into the crea mixture.

2 Pour into the mould or tin, cover wit a plate and put a weight on top. Freez for about 4 hours till firmly set.

3 Meanwhile, hull and pick over th raspberries. Reserve half the fruit an put the rest into a bowl with the caste sugar and liqueur and leave to macerat for 15 minutes.

4 Put into a saucepan and stir over a lo heat till the sugar dissolves. Pour int a bowl, allow to cool, then chill fo 2 hours.

5 Dip the mould or tin into hot water fo 10 seconds and turn the timbale ou on to a serving dish. Score the side with a fork and decorate with th reserved raspberries. Serve the rasp berry and liqueur sauce separately.

Below: Timbale aux framboises – exciting ice cream dish with a liqueur-laced sauce

Baked Alaska

An impressive American baked ice cream dessert, and amazingly simple to make. A perfect baked Alaska needs last-minute assembly for the meringue to be a light golden colour and the ice cream inside to be firm so it doesn't melt and make the cake soggy. To avoid this, have the ice cream as hard as possible before putting the dessert together. Although stale sponge cake can be used, freshly baked sponge gives a better result

DESSERT   Serves 6

Overall timing 30 minutes plus 1 hour marination

Equipment 2 bowls, saucepan, baking tray, palette knife or piping bag and star nozzle

Freezing Not recommended

INGREDIENTS

oz		
	Glacé fruit	125g
tbsp	Kirsch or other liqueur	4×15ml
	Egg whites	6
2oz	Icing sugar	350g
	Pinch of cream of tartar	
	Pinch of salt	
tbsp	Lemon juice	15ml
	Sponge cake	1
pint	Block of vanilla ice cream	560ml

METHOD

1. Put glacé fruit and liqueur in a bowl and chill for 1 hour.
2. Preheat the oven to 475F (240C) Gas 9. Put egg whites, sifted icing sugar, cream of tartar, salt and lemon juice in a bowl placed over a pan of hot water. Whisk over a very gentle heat till stiff and dry.
3. Cut sponge cake in half lengthways. Place 1 layer on baking tray. Spoon fruit and liqueur over, then put ice cream on top. Cover with the other sponge layer.
4. Working quickly, pipe or spread whisked white all over cake, making sure all the ice cream is covered.
5. Dredge with a little icing sugar and bake in hot oven for 5 minutes or until meringue is golden. Serve immediately.

1 *Holding the cake firmly with one hand, cut in half lengthways, with a sharp knife*

2 *Place one cake half on a baking tray and spoon glacé fruit and liqueur over*

3 *Trim ice cream to same shape as cake if necessary and place on top of fruit*

4 *When the ice cream is in position, quickly cover with the other piece of sponge cake*

5 *Working quickly, spread stiffly whisked egg white over sides of cake and ice cream*

6 *Pipe or spread more of the egg white on top of the cake to cover it completely*

7 *To use up any remaining egg white, pipe decorative shapes round sides*

8 *Dredge with a little icing sugar before baking in a very hot oven for 5 minutes*

cream and sprinkle with chopp
almonds. Pipe swirls of Crème Chantil
on top and decorate with redcurran
Serve immediately with wafers.

Persimmon ice cream

An American favourite, persimmon ice cream is simple to prepare and makes an unusual dessert. The fruit is peeled, mashed with sugar and lemon juice and added to whipped cream, then frozen till firm

DESSERT   Serves

Overall timing 30 minutes plus freezing

Equipment 2 bowls, freezer tray

Freezing Freeze in tray and cover.
Freezer life: 2 months. To use: soften in fridge for 30 minutes before serving

INGREDIENTS

4	Ripe persimmons	4
2 tbsp	Caster sugar	2×15ml
	Juice of 2 lemons	
¾ pint	Double cream	400ml

METHOD

1 Rub the persimmons all over with th back of a knife to loosen the skins. Usin a sharp knife and starting at the top the fruit, nick the skin and strip it awa from the flesh.
2 Chop the persimmons in a bowl an mash lightly. Add the sugar and lemo juice and mix well.
3 Whip the cream in a bowl till soft peak form and fold into the persimmon pul with a metal spoon.
4 Spread the mixture into a freezer tra and freeze for about 2 hours till mushy Tip the mixture into a bowl, beat we with wooden spoon and return to th freezer tray.
5 Return to the freezer and freeze ti firm. Serve in scoops with crisp biscuit or fan wafers.

Above: Redcurrant melba — summery mixture of redcurrants, nuts, cream and ice cream

Redcurrant melba

An enticing dessert which is very quick and simple to prepare and looks most effective in individual glasses. The ice cream and touch of sugar in the Crème Chantilly help to sweeten the redcurrants. If you prefer, poach them lightly in sugar syrup first

DESSERT   Serves 8

Overall timing 25 minutes

Equipment Bowl, piping bag, star nozzle, individual serving glasses

Freezing Not recommended

INGREDIENTS

1lb	Redcurrants	450g
2oz	Split almonds	50g
	Crème Chantilly (recipe page 26)	
2 pints	Vanilla ice cream	1.1 litres

METHOD

1 Wash and drain the redcurrants. Remove the stalks. Coarsely chop the almonds.
2 Prepare the Crème Chantilly according to the instructions on page 26 and put into a piping bag fitted with a star nozzle.
3 Reserve a few of the redcurrants, then divide the rest between chilled individual glasses. Top with cubes of ice

rawberry
e cream

really superb ice cream. If you
e, reserve some of the berries,
ll and quarter them and mix into
e frozen purée after whisking

SSERT   Serves 6–8

erall timing 20 minutes plus freezing

uipment Blender, nylon sieve, 2
wls, 2lb (900g) loaf tin

ezing Freeze in tin, cover and label.
ezer life: 2 months. To use: soften
fridge for 30 minutes before serving

GREDIENTS

lb	Strawberries	800g
	Juice of ½ a lemon	
z	Caster sugar	175g
int	Double cream	400ml

*ow: Strawberry ice cream — serve on its
n or surrounded with fresh strawberries*

METHOD

1 Wipe and hull the strawberries and
place in blender with the lemon juice.
Blend to a purée, then rub through a
nylon sieve into a bowl. Add the sugar
and mix thoroughly.
2 Whip the cream till soft peaks form, then
fold into the purée. Pour into the loaf
tin and freeze for 1½ hours.
3 Turn the mixture into a bowl and whisk
till smooth. Return to the tin and freeze
till firm. Remove from the freezer and
place in the fridge to soften for 30
minutes before serving.

Fraises Melba

A light, luscious colourful dessert
that's perfect for a summer party —
don't stint on the whipped cream

DESSERT   Serves 4

Overall timing 20 minutes

Equipment Nylon sieve, saucepan,
4 individual serving glasses, bowl

Freezing Not recommended

INGREDIENTS

12oz	Strawberries	350g
2 tbsp	Strawberry jam	2×15ml
1 tbsp	Kirsch	15ml
¼ pint	Double cream	150ml
¼ teasp	Almond essence	1.25ml
	Vanilla ice cream	

METHOD

1 Hull and wipe the strawberries. Reserve
12 firm ones and press the rest through
a nylon sieve into a pan. Add the jam
and Kirsch, and stir over a gentle heat
till smooth. Rub through a sieve into
4 serving glasses. Leave to cool.
2 Meanwhile, whip the cream till stiff
peaks form, fold in the essence.
3 Top the strawberry purée with a scoop
of ice cream and a swirl of cream and
decorate with the reserved strawberries.
Serve immediately with crisp biscuits.

VARIATIONS

Replace the almond essence with 1oz
(25g) toasted nuts, or use chocolate dots
and serve with chocolate ice cream.

*Below: Fraises Melba — a Kirsch flavoured
strawberry purée with almond-laced cream*

Chocolate and chestnut bombe

A perfect taste treat – two flavours of ice cream sprinkled with nuts

DESSERT   Serves 10

Overall timing 1 hour plus 8 hours freezing

Equipment Large bowls, saucepans, freezer trays, 4 pint (2.2 litre) mould or freezerproof bowl

Press the frozen-till-mushy chestnut ice cream on to sides and base of the mould

Pour fruit ice cream into centre, smooth top. Freeze till firm before unmoulding

Freezing Freeze in mould or bowl. Co with foil, place in a polythene bag, se label and freeze. Freezer life: 3 month To use: complete Step 8

INGREDIENTS

6	Egg yolks	6
6oz	Caster sugar	175g
1½ pints	Milk	850m.
1	Vanilla pod	1
3½oz	Plain dessert chocolate	100g
8oz	Can of sweetened chestnut purée	225g
4oz	Chopped glacé fruits	125g
2 tbsp	Kirsch or brandy	2×15
¾ pint	Double cream	400m
2	Egg whites	2
1oz	Chopped pistachios	25g

METHOD

1 Put egg yolks and sugar into a la bowl and mix thoroughly. Heat n with vanilla pod till almost boili remove pod and pour milk on to y mixture stirring constantly.

2 Place bowl over a pan of simmer water and cook, stirring, for 10 minu till custard coats back of spoon.

3 Break up chocolate into a bowl o simmering water and stir till melt Remove bowl, beat in chestnut pur

4 Strain two-thirds of custard into che nut mixture, fold in carefully w metal spoon. Stir glacé fruits, liqu into remaining custard. Leave till cc

5 Whip cream till it holds its shape. F two-thirds into chestnut custard, o third into fruit custard. Whisk whites till stiff but not dry, fold i fruit custard. Pour both into free trays and fast freeze for about 2 hou

6 Remove both ice creams from freezer, turn into separate bowls a beat each with a wooden spoon to bre down large ice crystals. Return freezer and freeze till mushy (abc 1 hour). Chill mould or bowl.

7 Spread chestnut ice cream over base and sides of the mould or bo packing it firmly and smoothing it w the back of a spoon to leave a space the centre. Spoon the fruit ice cre into the centre, pressing it in gen Smooth top and return to freezer ov night or for at least 4 hours till fir

8 Transfer bombe to the fridge for minutes to soften slightly before se ing. Dip the mould in hot water fo few seconds. Place the serving dish top and invert the plate and mou Remove mould, sprinkle with pistachi

Left: Chocolate and chestnut bombe – a delicious standby for your freezer

Fruit sauces, served hot or cold, are a quick and impressive way of dressing up desserts. They are delicious poured over ice cream and topped with a few nuts.

Melba sauce One of the most famous fruit sauces created by Escoffier in honour of Dame Nellie Melba, the celebrated Australian opera singer. Press 8oz (225g) fresh raspberries through a sieve into a small pan. Add 1oz (25g) sugar and 3 tbsp (3×15ml) redcurrant jelly. Bring to the boil, stirring. Blend 2 teasp (2×5ml) arrowroot with 1 tbsp (15ml) cold water and stir into the sauce. Heat gently, without boiling, till mixture thickens and clears. Sieve and allow to cool before serving with peach halves and ice cream.

Apricot sauce Put ½ pint (300ml) water and 4oz (125g) sugar in a pan. Heat gently, without stirring, until sugar dissolves. Bring to the boil and simmer gently for about 10 minutes. Leave to cool. Place in blender with 8oz (225g) stoned ripe apricots and blend for a few seconds till reduced to a purée. Serve cold or heat gently for 5 minutes and serve.

Berry sauce Make as for apricot sauce above, using 1lb (450g) fresh or frozen hulled strawberries, blackberries or raspberries instead of the apricots.

Orange or lemon sauce Using a potato peeler, pare the rind from 1 orange and shred finely. Simmer in boiling water for 5 minutes, then drain and rinse in cold water. Sieve 8 tbsp (8×15ml) each of orange marmalade and apricot jam into pan. Add 3 tbsp (3×15ml) orange-flavoured liqueur and the rind. Heat gently and serve hot or cold. For lemon sauce, make as above, but use 1 large or 2 small lemons instead of the orange, and lime instead of orange marmalade. All these sauces can be kept, covered, in the fridge for up to a week. They also freeze well. Pack into rigid container or divide between small cartons in meal-size amounts. Cover, label and freeze. Freezer life: 1 year. To use: thaw in fridge overnight, or heat gently from frozen, stirring occasionally.

Deluxe ice cream

Condensed milk gives an extra smoothness to this creamy ice, and its natural sweetness is tempered with the addition of lemon juice

Above: Pistachio ice cream – follow the recipe on page 5 for Basic vanilla ice cream to the end of Step 4. Add 4oz (125g) blanched pistachios pounded to a paste and a few drops of green food colouring to the whipped cream, then continue with Steps 5, 6 and 7. Freeze in a rectangular container so the ice cream can be sliced

Below: Deluxe ice cream – party dessert

DESSERT   Serves 4

Overall timing 10 minutes plus chilling time

Equipment 2 bowls, freezer tray

Freezing See method. Freezer life: 3 months. To use: remove from freezer 10 minutes before serving

INGREDIENTS

14oz	Can of sweetened condensed milk	397g
4 tbsp	Lemon juice	4×15ml
¼ pint	Carton of single cream	150ml
2	Egg whites	2

METHOD

1 Pour condensed milk into a small bowl. Stir in lemon juice and cream, mixing till well combined.
2 In another bowl, whisk egg whites till stiff, then gradually fold the condensed milk and cream mixture into the whisked egg whites.
3 Pour into freezer trays and freeze till firm. Thaw till soft. Serve with wafers.

Fruity sorbet

Choose your favourite fruit for this easy to make sorbet

DESSERT　　　　　　Serves 4

Overall timing 20 minutes plus freezing

Equipment Saucepan, freezer trays, 2 bowls

Freezing See Method

INGREDIENTS

3oz	Caster sugar	75g
7fl oz	Water	200ml
½ pint	Puréed fruit	300ml
2 tbsp	Lemon juice	2×15ml
2	Egg whites	2

METHOD

1 Put the sugar and water into a pan and heat gently, stirring occasionally, until sugar dissolves. Bring to the boil and simmer for about 10 minutes. Remove from heat and leave to cool.
2 Mix the sugar syrup with the puréed fruit and lemon juice. Turn into freezer tray and freeze for 3 hours, mashing from time to time with a fork to break up crystals.
3 Whisk egg whites in a bowl till stiff. Remove fruit mixture from freezer, turn into another bowl and whisk. Carefully fold whisked whites into fruit mixture.
4 Return to freezer tray only until stiff enough to serve. Alternatively make sorbet in advance and allow to thaw for 15 minutes at room temperature before eating.

Pêche Melba

The famous fruit dessert created by Escoffier in honour of Dame Nellie Melba the celebrated opera singer. Always use fresh fruit, not canned, so you achieve the authentic taste

DESSERT　　　　　　Serves 4

Overall timing 25 minutes plus cooling

Equipment 2 saucepans, 4 individual glass dishes, nylon sieve, ice cream scoop

Freezing Not recommended

INGREDIENTS

4	Ripe peaches	4
½ pint	Water	300ml
5oz	Sugar	150g
1	Vanilla pod	1
8oz	Raspberries	225g
1 pint	Vanilla ice cream	560ml

METHOD

1 Skin and halve the peaches. Remove the stones. Put the water, 3oz (75g) of the sugar and the vanilla pod into a saucepan and stir over gentle heat till the sugar dissolves.
2 Bring to the boil, add the peach halves and cook gently for 2 minutes, turning them once. Remove from the heat and leave to cool completely in the syrup. Put glasses in fridge to chill.
3 Wipe and hull the raspberries. Put into a saucepan with the remaining sugar and heat gently, stirring till the sugar dissolves. Remove from the heat, cool slightly, then rub through a nylon sieve. Leave purée to cool completely.
4 Put scoops of ice cream into chilled dishes and top each with 2 peach halves. Spoon the raspberry purée over and serve immediately.

Iced strawberry tartlets

Dainty little tartlets filled with ice cream and berries and topped with a sherry and gooseberry sauce

DESSERT　　　　　　Serves

Overall timing 40 minutes

Equipment Baking tray, 4×3 inch (7.5cm) tartlet dishes, saucepan, sieve

Freezing Not recommended

INGREDIENTS

6oz	Sweet flan pastry (recipe page 71)	175g
4oz	Gooseberry jam	125g
2 tbsp	Sherry	2×15m
12oz	Strawberries	350g
1 pint	Italian-style vanilla ice cream or lemon sorbet	560ml

METHOD

1 Preheat the oven to 375F (190C) Gas Put baking tray in oven to heat.
2 Divide the pastry into 4. Put a quart into each tartlet dish and press in shape. Prick each base with a fork a place on heated baking tray. Bake ju above the centre of the oven for abo 25 minutes till crisp and golden.
3 Remove from the oven and leave cool completely. Meanwhile, put t jam and sherry into a saucepan a heat gently till melted. Sieve into sauceboat and leave to cool.
4 Hull and wipe the strawberries. Cut quarter of them in half lengthways, p the rest into a serving dish.
5 Arrange the tartlets on a serving dis Put a scoop of ice cream or sorbet in each and decorate with halved stra berries. Serve immediately with rema ing strawberries and gooseberry sau

Right: Iced strawberry tartlets — serve at once so the ice cream doesn't start to melt

lmond ice cream

s Italian ice cream, which can
made well in advance and stored
a freezer, can be served as it is or
h crushed praline (see page 16)
almond tuiles (see this page)

SERT   Serves 4–6

erall timing 45 minutes plus freezing
e

ipment Jug or bowl, pestle and
rtar, 2 saucepans, plastic mould or
ys for freezing

ezing Put in plastic mould or tray.
ap, label and freeze. Freezer life:
nonths. To use: remove from freezer
l leave in fridge for a short while to
en

GREDIENTS

	Almonds, with skins	125g
l oz	Milk	800ml
	Egg yolks	7
	Caster sugar	175g
	A few drops of almond essence	

THOD

Blanch the almonds then crush them
finely in a mortar with a pestle adding a
few drops of cold water to prevent the
almond oil from separating. (Alterna-
ively, grind almonds to a fine powder
n a coffee grinder).
Put the almonds and cold milk into a
saucepan and leave to soak for about
15 minutes.
Place saucepan on a low heat and
bring to the boil. Remove from heat
and strain. Keep warm.
In another saucepan, beat together the
egg yolks and sugar until pale and
creamy. Gradually add in the strained
milk mixture, beating well.
Put on a very low heat and stir continuously with a wooden spoon. Do
not boil. When the cream begins to
coat the spoon, remove from heat, add
essence and strain again, this time into
a plastic mould or tray. Cover so that
mould or tray is airtight and leave for
at least 20 minutes. When cold, place
in freezer. After an hour, remove and
mash ice cream with a fork to break up
crystals. Cover and refreeze till ready
to serve.

Above: Almond ice cream – two stages in the making are shown below. Left: blanched
almonds are crushed in a mortar. Right: seven egg yolks are separated into a bowl

Tuiles

Light-as-air, crisp and crunchy
biscuits from France. For success, the
eggs must be at room temperature
and not straight from the fridge

CONFECTIONERY   Makes about 10

Overall timing 40 minutes

Equipment 2 baking trays, mixing bowl,
palette knife or egg slice, rolling-pin

Freezing Not recommended

Storage Airtight tin

INGREDIENTS

2	Egg whites	2
3½oz	Caster sugar	100g
2oz	Plain flour	50g
2oz	Butter	50g
	A few drops of almond essence	
2oz	Flaked almonds	50g

METHOD

1 Grease and flour 2 baking trays and
set oven at 400F (200C) Gas 6.
2 Put egg whites into a bowl and whisk
until frothy, not stiff.
3 Whisk in sugar a little at a time. Sieve
the flour and melt the butter and
carefully fold them into egg mixture
with remaining ingredients.
4 Drop half teaspoonfuls of mixture on to
baking trays, leaving large gaps as the
mixture will spread during cooking.
Flatten each one slightly with a fork
to form a round disc.
5 Bake in the centre of the oven for
about 8 minutes. The biscuits should
be golden with a brown edge.
6 Using a palette knife or egg slice,
carefully remove each biscuit and place
over a rolling-pin.
7 When cool and crisp, remove from
rolling-pin and store (see left).

TO SERVE

Use to accompany ice creams and cold
desserts.

Cold desserts

Light and fresh to finish a meal, fruity, creamy desserts are just right.
Make them ahead to chill in the refrigerator, or whip them up at the
last moment, for the perfect way to trouble free entertaining.

Almond and cherry snowballs

The luscious sauce lifts this rice dessert into a special class

DESSERT   Serves 4

Overall timing 1½ hours

Equipment 2 saucepans, bowl, small moulds

Freezing Not recommended

INGREDIENTS

½ pint	Milk	300ml
1oz	Butter	25g
2oz	Granulated sugar	50g
	Pinch of salt	
3oz	Pudding rice	75g
2 teasp	Gelatine	2×5ml
¼ pint	Carton of double cream	150ml
¼ teasp	Vanilla essence	1.25ml
2oz	Chopped almonds	50g
2 tbsp	Kirsch	2×15ml
10½oz	Can of red cherries	298g
3 tbsp	Lemon juice	3×15ml
2 teasp	Arrowroot	2×5ml
	Red food colouring	
¼ teasp	Almond essence	1.25ml

METHOD

1 Put milk, butter, sugar and salt in a saucepan and bring to the boil. Stir in rice and simmer gently, uncovered, for 20–30 minutes till soft, creamy.
2 Meanwhile, mix gelatine in a cup with 2 tbsp (2×15ml) cold water. Leave to go firm, then put cup in saucepan of hot water and heat gently till gelatine dissolves. Whisk cream till stiff.
3 When rice is cooked, plunge pan into cold water to cool a little, then mix in gelatine, vanilla, almonds and half the Kirsch. Fold in cream.
4 Lightly oil moulds and fill with the rice mixture. Place in fridge to set (30 minutes to 1 hour).
5 Meanwhile, make the sauce. Drain cherries and place juice in saucep with lemon juice, arrowroot blend with a little water, a few drops of colouring and almond essence. Bri to boil, stirring. Remove from he stir in cherries, rest of Kirsch. Co
6 Run knife round edges of rice, th immerse moulds up to rim in very water for few seconds. Invert on individual serving dishes and spo over the cooled cherry sauce.

Above: Almond and cherry snowballs

PRUNES IN MADEIRA

Put 12oz (350g) plump prunes into a bowl. Cover with warm water and leave to soak for 1 hour. Put ½ pint (300ml) each of Madeira and water into a saucepan with 3 tbsp (3×15ml) caster sugar, a pared strip of orange rind, a 2 inch (5cm) piece of cinnamon stick and stir over a gentle heat till the sugar dissolves. Bring to the boil, cover and simmer for about 15 minutes. Drain the prunes, add to the syrup and simmer for 10 minutes. Discard the orange rind and cinnamon, pour into a serving dish and leave to cool. Cover and chill overnight. Serve with whipped cream and shortbread fingers.   **Serves 4**

avarois aux fraises

avarois is a cold, moulded cream
ssert – enriched in this case
h puréed strawberries. The name
a bit of a mystery – some people
ieve the dish was named by a
nch chef in honour of Bavaria,
ers claim it originated there

SSERT   Serves 6

erall timing 50 minutes plus chilling

iipment 7 inch (18cm) charlotte
uld, 3 bowls, 2 saucepans, nylon
ve, piping bag with star nozzle

ezing Prepare to end of Step 5, cover
uld with foil, overwrap, seal, label
l freeze. Freezer life: 3 months.
use: thaw in mould for 3–4 hours
room temperature. Complete Step 6

ow: Bavarois aux fraises – a rich and
ressive dessert for a special occasion

INGREDIENTS

2	Egg yolks	2
3oz	Caster sugar	75g
½ pint	Milk	300ml
1 tbsp	Lemon juice	15ml
1 tbsp	Water	15ml
1 tbsp	Powdered gelatine	15ml
1lb	Ripe strawberries	450g
½ pint	Carton of double cream	284ml
	Pink food colouring (optional)	

METHOD

1 Lightly oil the charlotte mould. Put the egg yolks and sugar into a bowl and beat with a wooden spoon till well mixed. Heat the milk till almost boiling, then pour it in a thin stream on to the yolks, stirring constantly.

2 Place the bowl over a pan of simmering water and cook gently, stirring, till the mixture thickens and will coat the back of a spoon – do not boil. Remove from the heat and leave to cool, stirring occasionally to prevent a skin forming.

3 Put the lemon juice and water into a small bowl, sprinkle the gelatine on top and leave to sponge. Place bowl in a pan of simmering water and stir till gelatine dissolves. Leave to cool slightly.

4 Wipe and hull the strawberries. Reserve a few for decoration and rub the rest through a nylon sieve into the custard. Pour the gelatine into the fruit custard in a thin stream and fold in with a metal spoon. Chill till syrupy and beginning to set.

5 Whip half the cream till it forms soft peaks. Fold into the fruit custard with a metal spoon, adding a few drops of pink food colouring if using. Pour into the mould and smooth the top. Chill for at least 4 hours till firm.

6 Run a knife round the edge of the mould and turn the bavarois out on to a serving dish. Whip the remaining cream till stiff and put into a piping bag fitted with a star nozzle. Pipe the cream on to the bavarois. Decorate with the reserved strawberries and serve immediately with shortbread fingers.

Oranges à la turque

The Turks are well known for their sweet tooth, and the sugary syrup used here is a traditional feature of their pastries and desserts. Caramelized and spiked with Cointreau, it's used to macerate the oranges and gives them an exquisite flavour with a light kick

DESSERT Serves 4

Overall timing 30 minutes plus maceration

Equipment Potato peeler, saucepan, flat-bottom dish

Freezing Not recommended

INGREDIENTS

4	Large oranges	4
8oz	Caster sugar	225g
2	Cloves	2
12 fl oz	Water	350ml
3 tbsp	Cointreau	3×15ml
4	Crystallized violets	4

METHOD

1 Wash the oranges and pare the rind from 2 of them with a potato peeler. Shred rind into fine long strands and then blanch in boiling water for 5 minutes. Drain and rinse in cold water, then dry on kitchen paper.

2 Put the sugar into a saucepan with the cloves and water and heat, stirring, till sugar dissolves. Bring to the boil and boil rapidly, without stirring, till a golden caramel colour.

3 Meanwhile, cut away the peel and from the remaining oranges, collect any juice. Place oranges in flat-bott dish with shredded rind.

4 Remove caramel from the heat. C fully add the Cointreau and any ora juice, and stir over a low heat to diss the caramel. Pour over the oranges rind and leave to macerate for 3 ho turning the oranges and rind in caramel occasionally.

TO SERVE

Arrange the oranges on individual serv plates and spoon the caramel over. the shredded rind on to the oranges decorate each with a crystallized vic and an orange leaf, if liked. Eat wit knife and fork, and provide a spoon for caramel. Serve with pouring cream if lik

One way of preparing oranges is to cut a slice from top and bottom, so removing t pith. Place one cut end down and cut peel from sides with a serrated knife, holding the orange steady with a fork

To make the oranges easier to eat, slice across segments with a serrated knife, holding orange steady with a fork, and serve in slices. Or reassemble the sliced orange on a wooden cocktail stick

Left: Oranges à la turque — an impressiv dish that's a delight to serve and to eat

eufs à la neige

scious floating islands of
ached meringue topped with
amel – but don't make it more
n 2 hours ahead of time

SSERT   Serves 4–6

erall timing 40 minutes plus chilling
e

uipment 2 saucepans, 2 bowls, glass
ving bowl, wire rack

ezing Not recommended

*ow: Oeufs à la neige – snowy meringue,
tard and a light topping of caramel*

INGREDIENTS

1 pint	Milk	560ml
1	Vanilla pod	1
5	Eggs	5
	Pinch of salt	
5oz	Caster sugar	150g
2oz	Icing sugar	50g
2 tbsp	Water	2×15ml

METHOD

1 Slowly heat the milk in a saucepan
  with the vanilla pod. Separate the eggs.
  Mix egg yolks, salt and 3oz (75g) of the
  caster sugar in a bowl. Remove pod
  and mix milk into eggs.
2 Return to pan and, stirring constantly,
  slowly bring to just below   boiling
  point – the mixture will lightly coat
  the spoon. Do not boil.

3 Remove custard from heat and allow
  to cool slightly before pouring into
  serving bowl. Chill.
4 Heat a saucepan of water. Whisk egg
  whites till stiff, sprinkle with icing
  sugar and whisk well again.
5 Using 2 soup spoons, make egg shapes
  of the egg white. Carefully lower a
  few at a time on to the simmering
  water and leave for 15 seconds on one
  side, 10 seconds on the other.
6 Remove egg shapes from pan with a
  draining spoon and place on a wire
  rack. Do not let them touch. When all
  are cooked and dried, carefully place
  the egg shapes on the custard.
7 Dissolve remaining sugar in water in
  a small saucepan and boil till it turns
  to caramel. Pour over the egg shapes
  and serve immediately.

Cream cheese moulds

From Brittany and Russia come these two recipes for uncooked, pressed curd or cream cheese dishes. Crémets are traditional to Brittany, where they are served as a dessert with soft summer fruits. Paska, which is eaten in many Baltic countries as well as the USSR, is prepared at the end of Lent to be eaten at the Easter breakfast, and the only decoration permitted are the letters XB – Christ is risen. This is stamped into the top part of the special wooden mould which is used to form the shape, though the characters can be formed with dried fruit when turned out of the mould

Above: Crémets – heart-shaped when made in the traditional crémets moulds at Brittany

Crémets

DESSERT   Serves 4

Overall timing 10 minutes plus 24 hours draining time

Equipment 2 bowls, muslin, moulds

Freezing Not recommended

INGREDIENTS

2	Egg whites	2
	Pinch of salt	
½ pint	Carton of double cream	284ml
12oz	Curd or cream cheese	350g
2 teasp	Lemon juice	2×5ml
1 tbsp	Caster sugar	15ml
8oz	Fresh or frozen raspberries	225g
	Caster sugar	
	Single cream	

METHOD

1 In a bowl, whisk the egg whites with salt until soft peaks form. Add sugar and continue to beat until stiff.
2 If using curd cheese put through a sieve first to even the consistency. Add the cream and beat until smooth and thick.
3 Fold the egg whites and sugar lightly into the cheese, then fold lemon juice through mixture.
4 Line small crémet moulds (or cream cartons pierced several times in the base) with muslin. Spoon in the mixture and place on a plate covered with 3 or 4 thicknesses of kitchen paper to drain. Cover and leave 1 full day in fridge, changing paper once.

TO SERVE

Turn out moulds carefully just before serving. Sprinkle with extra caster sugar and serve with raspberries or any other soft fruit and single cream which can be lightly sweetened with vanilla essence.

Paska

DESSERT   Serves

Overall timing 30 minutes plus drain time

Equipment Sieve, 2 bowls, sterilized large clay flower pot or 8 small ones (see Cook's know-how) or 1¾ pint (1 litre) mould

Freezing Pack in foil or film, overwrap label and freeze. Freezer life: 2 months To use: thaw overnight in fridge

INGREDIENTS

1lb	Curd or cream cheese	450g
2oz	Sultanas	50g
3oz	Softened butter	75g
3oz	Caster sugar	75g
3	Egg yolks	3
8fl oz	Carton of double cream	227ml
2oz	Chopped almonds	50g

METHOD

1 If using curd cheese, place it in a clo tea-towel and squeeze out moistu Leave overnight to dry. If using cre cheese, press through a sieve.
2 Put sultanas in a bowl and cover w boiling water. Soak for 30 minutes plump, then drain and dry on kitch paper.
3 Cream butter, sugar and egg yolks a mixing bowl. Gradually add cheese, cream, sultanas and almon
4 Line sterilized flower pot or pots w butter muslin or a cloth, and fill to top with the creamed mixture.
5 Put a plate or saucers on top and h down with a weight. Place in a bc and leave to drain for 24 hours. Tu on to a plate. Serve sliced with cr biscuits or fruit.

cook's know-how

Porous clay flower pots (large or th smaller seedling pots for individual servings) make ideal moulds for dishes such as Russian Paska or Breton Crémets where it is important that the liquid drains out To sterilize pots before use, place in saucepan, and cover with cold water. Bring to the boil and simmer for at least 5 minutes. Remove from pan with tongs and place in a just warm oven till ready to use.

The ingredients for making paska — cheese can be curd or cream

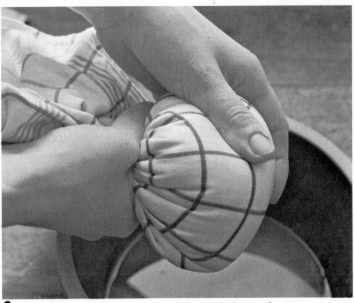

2 Squeeze excess moisture out of the curd cheese if using

Mix butter, sugar and yolks, then other ingredients

4 Line the pot or pots with muslin and add creamed mixture

Cover pot with a plate and weight and leave for 24 hours

6 Turn paska out to serve — it retains its pot shape

Brazilian fool

A light and creamy, soufflé-type dessert that is made with bananas as well as blackberries

DESSERT   Serves 6

Overall timing 45 minutes

Equipment 2 bowls, small saucepan

Freezing Not recommended

INGREDIENTS

4 tbsp	Custard powder	4×15ml
	Pinch of salt	
4 tbsp	Caster sugar	4×15ml
1 pint	Milk	560ml
1	Large egg	1
½oz	Butter	15g
2	Large bananas	2
3 tbsp	Lemon juice	3×15ml
	Grated nutmeg	
	Vanilla essence	
8oz	Blackberries	225g
¼ pint	Carton of double cream	150ml

Below: Brazilian fool – a delicious dessert that must be served as soon as it's made

METHOD

1 Mix custard powder, salt and half the sugar with a little of the cold milk. Place rest of milk in saucepan and heat. When almost boiling, remove from heat and quickly stir in custard/milk mixture. Return pan to gentle heat and stir until custard thickens.
2 Remove pan from heat and leave custard to cool slightly. Separate egg. Stir yolk and butter into custard.
3 Peel and finely chop bananas and sprinkle with lemon juice. Stir into custard with a little grated nutmeg, a few drops of vanilla essence and the rest of the sugar. Cool custard quickly by standing pan in cold water. Stir occasionally to prevent skin forming.
4 Whisk egg white till very stiff and fold into cold custard. Wash and dry blackberries and add most to custard. Divide mixture between 6 glasses.
5 Whip cream and spread over custard. Decorate with remaining blackberries and serve immediately.

Blackberry special

An impressive dessert to bring a meal to a splendid conclusion. It's fruity, tangy and crunchy – a dish to suit all tastes, in fact

DESSERT   Serves 6–8

Overall timing 4 hours including chilling but not cooling time

Equipment 2 bowls, 9 inch (23cm) loose-bottom flan dish 2 inches (5cm) deep, or springform tin, baking tray, piping bag and large rose nozzle

Freezing Not recommended

INGREDIENTS

	Base	
6oz	Plain flour	150g
2	Egg yolks	2
3oz	Caster sugar	75g
3oz	Butter	75g
¼ teasp	Salt	1.25ml
	Filling	
1lb	Blackberries	450g
2oz	Candied peel	50g
	Topping	
3	Egg whites	3
6oz	Caster sugar	175g
6oz	Ground almonds	175g
1 teasp	Grated lemon rind	5ml
¼ teasp	Cinnamon	1.25ml
2oz	Flaked almonds	25g

METHOD

1 To make base, sieve flour into a mixi bowl. Make a well in the centre a add egg yolks, sugar, small flakes chilled butter and salt. Mix well th knead to a pliable dough. Cover a place in the fridge for 2 hours.
2 Preheat oven to 375F (190C) Gas Remove dough from fridge, roll c and use to line flan ring (stand it baking tray). The dough should ⅛ inch (3mm) above the rim of the ri Prick base and, to prevent si collapsing, line closely with foil, pr sing it against the dough. Fill w dried beans and bake in the middle the oven for 15 minutes.
3 To make filling, rinse blackberries a dry on kitchen paper. Remove fl from oven and reduce heat to 30 (150C) Gas 2. Remove foil and bea Add blackberries to flan and sprin with candied peel.

Left: Blackberry special — an impressive mixture of tastes and textures
Below: Baroness pears — sweet and simple combination of fruit and jelly

To make topping, whip egg whites until very stiff. Fold in sugar a little at a time, and then ground almonds, lemon rind and cinnamon. Put 3 tbsp (3×15ml) of the mixture in a piping bag fitted with a large rose nozzle. Spread the remainder over blackberries. Sprinkle edges of flan with flaked almonds and decorate the top with swirls of piped egg white.

Bake flan in oven for 1 hour 10 minutes. If after 40 minutes the top is browning too much, cover with foil.

Remove from the oven and cut flan into wedges before it cools. When cold, remove flan ring and serve.

ARIATION

> make the three separate layers of is dessert stand out, make a flat base ith the dough instead of taking it up e sides of the dish or tin.

Baroness pears

A stylish dessert that combines fruit with a wine-flavoured jelly

DESSERT   Serves 4

Overall timing $1\frac{1}{4}$ hours

Equipment 2 saucepans, 4 individual serving glasses, measuring jug

Freezing Not recommended

INGREDIENTS

4	Firm, ripe pears	4
3 tbsp	Lemon juice	3×15ml
3 tbsp	Caster sugar	3×15ml
4 teasp	Gelatine	4×5ml
$\frac{1}{2}$ pint	Red wine	300ml
8oz	Firm blackberries	225g
1oz	Chopped almonds	25g

METHOD

1 Peel pears leaving stalks on. Remove core from base end (optional).
2 Place pears upright in saucepan. Pour in $\frac{3}{4}$ pint (400ml) boiling water, add the lemon juice and sugar. Poach pears gently for 8 minutes.
3 Dissolve gelatine in 3 tbsp (3×15ml) of the wine by heating gently over a saucepan of boiling water.
4 Lift out pears from pan with a draining spoon and place in individual dishes. Strain $\frac{1}{2}$ pint (300ml) of the cooking liquor into measuring jug and stir in dissolved gelatine. Mix in remaining red wine and leave to cool.
5 Pour jelly around pears, and place in fridge till set.

TO SERVE

Wash and dry blackberries and place around pears. Sprinkle chopped almonds on top and serve with whipped cream.

Caramel bombe

A very rich concoction with cream in the caramel as well as the custardy centre of the bombe

DESSERT   Serves 6

Overall timing 25 minutes plus 5–6 hours chilling time

Equipment Saucepan, 7 inch (18cm) round mould or bowl, double saucepan, bowl, piping bag and large star nozzle

Freezing Not recommended

INGREDIENTS

	Caramel	
3oz	Sugar	75g
2 tbsp	Water	2×15ml
2 tbsp	Cream	2×15ml
	Cream	
4	Egg yolks	4
3 tbsp	Caster sugar	3×15ml
½ teasp	Vanilla essence	2.5ml
1 pint	Double cream	560ml
	Decoration	
6	Sponge fingers	6
1oz	Toasted chopped nuts	25g

METHOD

1 Heat sugar in a saucepan over moderate heat until golden brown. Stir in the water and cream and cook for a further 4 minutes until the caramel thickens.
2 Pour into a bowl or mould and rotate it to distribute the caramel over the base and sides. Plunge bowl into cold water to cool caramel.
3 To make the cream, heat egg yolks, 1 tbsp (15ml) of the caster sugar and the vanilla in the top of a double saucepan over a low heat. Whisk till foamy, then remove from heat and place top saucepan in cold water.
4 In a bowl, beat cream till stiff; add the sugar. Put aside 5 tbsp (5×15ml) of the sugared cream for decoration. Fold the rest into the egg yolks.
5 Remove mould or bowl from cold water. Put mixture into mould and leave in fridge for 5–6 hours.

TO SERVE

Immerse mould or bowl in hot water up to rim for 5–10 seconds, then turn bombe out on to serving plate. Put remaining cream into a piping bag with a large star nozzle. Decorate the bombe with cream, sponge fingers and toasted chopped nuts.

Above: Crème caramel — creamy custard topped with a deliciously soft caramel sauce

Crème caramel

The most favoured of the French desserts, and very easy to make

DESSERT   Serves 6

Overall timing 45 minutes

Equipment 2 saucepans, bowl, 6 small or a large mould, roasting tin

Freezing Not recommended

INGREDIENTS

1 pint	Milk	560ml
½	Vanilla pod	½
1	Piece lemon peel	1
4	Eggs	4
2oz	Caster sugar	50g
	Caramel	
4 tbsp	Caster sugar	4×15ml

METHOD

1 Preheat the oven to 350F (180C) Gas 4. Bring the milk, the vanilla pod and lemon peel to the boil in a saucepan. Remove from heat and lift out the vanilla pod and lemon peel.
2 In a bowl, beat eggs and sugar and pour in the hot milk, a little at a time, stirring constantly.
3 Melt the sugar for the caramel in a saucepan over a moderate heat till golden brown, then divide between the small moulds and turn them round so the caramel coats the bases and sides.
4 Strain the cream mixture into the moulds and place them in a roasting tin half-filled with hot water.
5 Bake for 45 minutes until set. Allow to cool in moulds and refrigerate before turning out.

Eggs and sugar are beaten together. then the vanilla and lemon-flavoured milk is stirred in gradually with a wooden spoon

The caramel is made by melting sugar over a low heat until it turns brown and is runny. Pour into large or small moulds and turn so caramel coats base and sides

You can either strain the egg and milk mixture into the moulds. or ladle it in. Place in a roasting tin half-filled with hot water and cook in oven till set

ramel melon
mpote

New Zealand, this would be made
h what is known as "pie melon" —
lon that's not ripe enough to eat
hout some cooking. The melon is
ched in syrup till tender but
l retaining its shape, then the
up is boiled till it becomes
amel and flavoured with orange-
ver water. As the dessert is
ved chilled, it can be made well
ad of time if necessary

SSERT   Serves 6

rall timing 30 minutes plus chilling

ipment Saucepan, serving bowl

ezing Pack in rigid container,
uring fruit is covered by syrup and
wing 1 inch (2.5cm) headspace.
er, seal and label. Freezer life: 1 year.
use: thaw overnight in fridge

REDIENTS

	Large underripe melon	1
oz	Water	200m
	Caster sugar	150g
	Grated rind of 1 orange	
asp	Orange-flower water	5ml

THOD

1 ut the melon in half and scoop out the
eeds. Remove the flesh from the rind
nd cut into neat chunks.
2 ut ¼ pint (150ml) of water, sugar and
rated orange rind in a saucepan and
eat gently, stirring, till sugar dissolves.
3ring to the boil. Add melon chunks
nd simmer for about 5 minutes till just
ender.
ift out melon chunks with a draining
poon and put in a serving bowl.
3oil the syrup till pale golden. Remove
rom the heat and carefully add re-
naining water and orange-flower
vater. Bring back to the boil, stirring.
temove from the heat and allow to
:ool. Pour over the melon and chill
efore serving.

Above: Redcurrant russe – piped cream and chocolate curls give an attractive finish

Redcurrant russe

Tart redcurrants and lemon perfectly
balance the sweetness of the other
ingredients in this splendid dish

DESSERT   Serves 6–8

Overall timing 50 minutes plus chilling

Equipment 3 bowls, 2lb (900g) loaf tin,
saucepan, piping bag and star nozzle

Freezing Complete to end of Step 6.
Cover with cling film, overwrap in
plastic, seal, label and freeze. Freezer
life: 2 months. To use: turn out and
thaw for 4–5 hours at room
temperature. Complete Steps 7 and 8

INGREDIENTS

1 tbsp	Kirsch or Cherry brandy	15ml
3 tbsp	Water	3×15ml
1 tbsp	Powdered gelatine	15ml
24	Sponge fingers	24
13¼oz	Can of condensed milk	383g
1	Lemon	1
8oz	Redcurrants	225g
½ pint	Carton of double cream	284ml
	Chocolate curls	

METHOD

1 Put the Kirsch and water into a small
bowl, sprinkle the gelatine over and
leave to sponge.
2 Meanwhile, base-line the tin. Arrange
sponge fingers over the base and
around sides, with sugared side against
the tin. Trim the ends level with the tin.
Roughly crush the trimmings and
reserve.
3 Stand the bowl of gelatine in a pan of
simmering water and stir till dissolved.
Leave to cool.
4 Meanwhile, put the condensed milk
into a bowl. Wash the lemon and grate
the rind into the milk. Squeeze out the
juice and beat into the milk with the
gelatine. Leave for 10 minutes.
5 Add crushed sponge finger trimmings
to mixture with picked over redcurrants. Whip half the cream till soft
peaks form and fold into the mixture
with a metal spoon.
6 Pour into the tin and smooth the top.
Chill for 2–3 hours till set.
7 Run a knife carefully round the edge of
the tin and turn out on to a serving dish.
Whip remaining cream, put into a
piping bag with a star nozzle and pipe
decoratively along the top.
8 Sprinkle the chocolate curls over and
serve immediately.

Strawberry milk ring

A mouthwatering dessert that tastes as good as it looks — the evaporated milk should be chilled for several hours to make sure it whisks up well

DESSERT Serves 6

Overall timing 30 minutes plus setting

Equipment 4 bowls, saucepan, 2 pint (1.1 litre) ring mould, piping bag, nozzle

Freezing Not recommended

INGREDIENTS

1	Lemon	1
5 teasp	Powdered gelatine	5×5ml
5 tbsp	Caster sugar	5×15ml
1	Large can of evaporated milk	1
½ pint	Buttermilk	300ml
	Pink food colouring	
1	Egg white	1
¼ pint	Carton of double cream	150ml
1lb	Fresh strawberries	450g

Below: Strawberry milk ring — a German dessert made with well chilled evaporated milk

METHOD

1 Grate the rind from the lemon and reserve. Squeeze out the juice and place in a small bowl. Sprinkle the gelatine over and leave to sponge.
2 Stand the bowl in a pan of simmering water and stir till gelatine has dissolved. Stir in the sugar. Remove from the heat and allow to cool slightly.
3 Pour the well-chilled evaporated milk into a large bowl and whisk till very thick and foamy. Whisk in the buttermilk and the gelatine mixture together with the reserved lemon rind and a few drops of food colouring.
4 Pour into the wetted mould and chill for 3–4 hours till set. Dip the mould up to the rim in hot water for a few seconds and turn out on to a serving plate.
5 Whisk the egg white till stiff but not dry. Whip the cream till stiff and fold into the whisked white. Hull the strawberries and pile half in the centre of the mould. Pipe the cream mixture on top and around the base of the mould. Decorate with the remaining strawberries and serve immediately.

Finnish maitokiiss

Here's a dessert that's simplicity itself, and can be made using ingredients from the storecupboar The contrast of a cold base and a hot sauce is always interesting — ring the changes with different jar or add a sauce made with fresh fr

DESSERT Serve

Overall timing 20 minutes plus chill

Equipment Saucepan

Freezing Not recommended

INGREDIENTS

2oz	Plain flour	50g
2oz	Caster sugar	50g
1½ pints	Milk	850m
	Jam sauce (below)	

METHOD

1 Put the flour and all but 1 tbsp (1 of the sugar into a heavy-based and gradually add the milk, stir with a wooden spoon to prevent lu forming.
2 Bring just to the boil, stirring constar Reduce heat and simmer for 10 minn stirring frequently.
3 Pour into a serving dish, sprinkle reserved sugar over the surface allow to cool. Chill for 2–3 hours be serving with hot jam sauce.

cook's know-how

When time is short or you're stuck for ideas, jam sauces are an excellent way of livening up desserts, adding colour and flavour They can be served, for example, with steamed, baked or milk puddings; spooned over ice cream or canned fruit; or served with omelettes, pancakes and waffles. To make a basic clear jam sauce, warm 4 tbsp (4×15ml) jam in a pan with ¼ pint (150ml) water. Blend 1 teasp (5ml) arrowroot with 1 tbs (15ml) water and stir in. Cook till sauce thickens and clears, then add 1 tbsp (15ml) lemon juice to counter act excessive sweetness. Sieve if liked For a thinner sauce, simply warm jam with lemon juice before using. Experiment with different flavour combinations, or try adding 1 tbsp (15ml) liqueur for extra taste.

Chestnut cups

Amazingly quick dessert with a clean, fresh fruit flavour. Chill all the ingredients (except the egg white which should be at room temperature) before you start

DESSERT   Serves 4

Overall timing 15 minutes plus chilling time

Equipment Bowls, whisk, grater

Freezing Not recommended

INGREDIENTS

8oz	Can of unsweetened chestnut purée	225g
2oz	Icing sugar	50g
¼ pint	Unsweetened apple juice	150ml
	Dessert apple	1
	Orange	1
¼ pint	Carton of whipping cream	150g
	Egg white	1
	Pinch of salt	
2oz	Chopped hazelnuts	50g

METHOD
1 All the ingredients (except egg white) should be very cold. Whisk the chestnut purée with the icing sugar.
2 Gradually add the apple juice, whisking until a soft, smooth consistency is obtained.
3 Peel apples, then grate into chestnut mixture. Grate orange peel. Stir into mixture. Spoon into 4 individual glasses or dishes. Chill.
4 Remove pith from oranges. Cut each into 8 segments, then cut across into 16 pieces.
5 Whisk the cream until thick. Whisk egg white and salt until it forms stiff peaks. Fold egg mixture into cream. Chill.
6 Just before serving sprinkle hazelnuts over the chestnut mixture. Decorate with orange pieces and cream.

Above: Charlotte aux marrons — made with chestnut purée and marrons glacés

Charlotte aux marrons

Definitely a superb dessert for chestnut lovers. It's very rich so the servings need only to be small. It's quite quick to make but needs chilling

DESSERT   Serves 8

Overall timing 30 minutes plus 3 hours chilling time

Equipment 6 inch (15cm) charlotte mould or deep, round cake tin, 2 bowls, cup, saucepan

Freezing Complete to end of Step 6. Freeze the charlotte in the mould then unmould and wrap in foil and label. Freezer life: 1 month. To use: unwrap and place on serving dish, then loosely cover and thaw at room temperature. Decorate as in Step 7

INGREDIENTS

½oz	Butter	15g
4fl oz	Whisky	125ml
2fl oz	Water	50ml
20	Sponge fingers	20
1lb	Can of sweetened chestnut purée	450g
4 teasp	Gelatine	4×5ml
¾ pint	Double cream	420ml
7oz	Chopped marrons glacés	250g
8	Marrons glacés	8

METHOD
1 Grease charlotte mould or deep cake tin.
2 Place half the whisky and the water in a bowl. Quickly dip sponge fingers into the whisky mixture so they absorb the liquid but do not disintegrate.
3 Line the base and sides of the mould or tin with the sponge fingers, placing the curved sides against the side of the mould or tin. Mix the chestnut purée with the remaining whisky.
4 In a cup mix the gelatine with 2 tbsp (2×15ml) cold water and leave to go firm. Place cup in a pan of hot water and heat gently until the gelatine has dissolved. Stir into the chestnut purée.
5 Whip the cream until thick. Fold two-thirds of it into the chestnut mixture, then half fill the lined mould. Sprinkle with the marrons glacés pieces. Add the remaining chestnut mixture.
6 Trim sponge fingers so they are level with the mould. Cover with a plate and a weight. Chill for at least 3 hours.
7 Put the mould into hot water for a few moments, then turn charlotte out on to a serving dish. Pipe or spread the remaining cream on top of the charlotte and serve immediately.

Canned fruits are a good standby for simple, but impressive desserts.
Glass desserts can be made in individual dishes and chilled. Drain a 15oz (425g) can of stoned fruit and put in a blender with 2 tbsp (2×15ml) of the syrup and blend till smooth. Sieve soft fruits after blending to remove seeds, then carefully fold one of the following into the purée: ¼ pint (150ml) double cream whisked to soft peaks; ¼ pint (150ml) chilled evaporated milk whisked till thick; instant dessert made up with ½ pint (300ml) milk; 15oz (425g) canned creamed rice (add food colouring if liked). Chill desserts, then serve with crisp biscuits. Or you can add to the blender: 1 jelly tablet melted in 3 tbsp (3×15ml) canned syrup, then added to ½ pint (300ml) of remaining syrup and ice water and set till syrupy; or 4oz (125g) marshmallows and 2 teasp (2×5ml) lemon juice.

Rodgrød med fløde

Delicious berry fruits of summer are combined in this delectable dessert from Denmark. As the fruits are gently cooked before being thickened, the dish could be made in winter with frozen fruit

DESSERT   Serves 6

Overall timing 20 minutes plus cooling and chilling

Equipment Saucepan, measuring jug, serving dish

Freezing Do not decorate. Cook, pour into rigid container, cover, label and freeze. Freezer life: 3 months. To use: thaw overnight in fridge, then decorate and serve.

Below: Rødgrød med fløde – a red fruit jelly popular in Denmark. The fruits are cooked till soft but still whole, then the juice is strained off and thickened. The dessert should be served chilled

INGREDIENTS

1½lb	Mixed soft fruit (raspberries, strawberries, blackcurrants, redcurrants, blackberries, loganberries)	700g
4oz	Caster sugar	125g
	Arrowroot	
1oz	Toasted flaked almonds (optional)	25g

METHOD

1 Wash and prepare fruit. Put into a saucepan and add enough water to just cover. Bring gently to the boil and simmer for about 5 minutes or until soft. Strain fruit and measure amount of juice. Place fruit in serving dish.

2 Return juice to pan, add sugar and heat gently till sugar dissolves.

3 Allowing 2 teasp (2×5ml) per pint (560ml) of fruit juice, measure out arrowroot and mix with a little cold water. Stir into pan and heat gently for 2 minutes, stirring constantly until slightly thickened and glossy. Do not boil.

4 Pour over fruit in serving dish, and leave to cool. Chill for 1 hour, then decorate with flaked almonds and serve with unsweetened whipped cream.

Italian loganberry custard

A typical Italian *spumone* — a light, soufflé-like dessert made by folding cream into a purée or custard base, then chilling in a mould till firm. All sorts of flavourings can be added — fruit, coffee or nuts for example. In this one, the smooth *crème pâtissière* base is flavoured with Maraschino, and coarsely chopped meringues are added to give a contrasting crunchiness. The dessert should be served well chilled and the sweetened loganberry purée poured over at the last minute

DESSERT Serves 6–8

Overall timing 30 minutes plus chilling

Equipment 2 bowls, round or rectangular mould with lid

Freezing Not recommended

INGREDIENTS

½ pint	Crème pâtissière (recipe page 71)	300ml
6	Small meringues	6
¾ pint	Double cream	400ml
2 tbsp	Maraschino	2×15ml
8oz	Loganberries	225g
3oz	Icing sugar	75g

METHOD
1 Make crème pâtissière according to recipe on page 71 and leave to cool.
2 Coarsely chop the meringues. Whip the cream and chill. When the crème is cold but not set, gently stir in crushed meringues, cream and Maraschino. Pour mixture into mould, cover with lid or damp greaseproof paper and chill for 2 hours or until set.
3 Meanwhile, hull and pick over loganberries, then press through a sieve into a bowl. Stir in icing sugar and mix well. Chill for 1 hour. Also chill the serving dish.
4 Dip mould in hot water to loosen custard and transfer to chilled serving dish. Pour over loganberry purée. Serve immediately with Crème Chantilly (see page 26).

Right: Italian loganberry custard — cut into slices and serve with Crème Chantilly

Loganberry and cream flan

Fresh or canned loganberries can be used as the filling for the sweet pastry case in this recipe. Chill and cut into slices to serve

DESSERT Serves 8

Overall timing 30 minutes

Equipment 9 inch (23cm) flan dish or tin, saucepan, bowl

Freezing Omit cream. Wrap in foil and place in polythene bag. Seal, label and freeze. Freezer life: 1 year. To use: unwrap and thaw at room temperature for 4–6 hours, then decorate with whipped cream

INGREDIENTS

	Sweet flan pastry (recipe page 71)	
1lb	Stewed or canned loganberries	450g
½oz	Butter	15g
1oz	Cornflour	25g
	Salt	
½ pint	Carton of whipping cream	284ml

METHOD
1 Prepare pastry (made with 8oz/225g flour). Use to line flan tin and bake blind.
2 If using stewed loganberries, reserve 4fl oz (120ml) of the juices; if using canned, reserve same amount of syrup.
3 Melt the butter till frothy in a saucepan. Blend cornflour with reserved juice or syrup, then stir into butter with a pinch of salt. Bring to the boil, stirring constantly, and cook until thickened, (about 5 minutes).
4 Remove from heat, stir in loganberries and leave to cool.
5 Spread loganberry sauce on to base of cold flan. Whip cream in a bowl until stiff, then spoon or pipe over filling.

VARIATIONS
Raspberry or other raspberry/blackberry hybrids can be used in this recipe instead of loganberries.

If you only have about 8oz (225g) fresh loganberries available and don't want to open a can, you can make up the amount of fruit to 1lb (450g) with apples. Peel, core and slice 3 large cooking apples and cook gently with 1 tbsp (15ml) lemon juice till reduced to a pulp; or bake apples in the oven at 375F (190C) Gas 5 for 25 minutes, then scoop out the flesh. Mix apples and loganberries together well, use to fill flan case and decorate as above.

Above: Egyptian fruit salad

Egyptian fruit salad

A delicious mix of dried fruit makes this unusual dessert called *khoshaf* which is popular in Egypt

DESSERT   Serves 6

Overall timing 15 minutes plus 48 hours soaking

Equipment Shallow dish, bowl

Freezing Not recommended

INGREDIENTS

8oz	Dried apricots	225g
4oz	Stoned prunes	125g
2oz	Seedless raisins	50g
4oz	Dried figs	125g
2oz	Flaked almonds	50g
1oz	Pistachio nuts	25g
2oz	Amardine	50g
½ pint	Water	300ml
1oz	Caster sugar	25g
1 tbsp	Orange flower water	15ml
2 teasp	Rose flower water	2×5ml

METHOD
1 Place the dried fruit in a shallow dish, halving the figs if very large. Sprinkle nuts over.
2 Soften the amardine in the water and add the sugar and flower waters. Pour over fruit.
3 Place in fridge for 48 hours, stirring occasionally. Serve very cold* with crisp biscuits or single cream.

*Place the serving dish in another dish filled with ice cubes and fresh grapes – to refresh the palate after the dessert course.

56

queur trifle

eliciously sweet trifle with a
ety of different flavours and
ours. The liqueur is used to
sten the halved trifle sponges

SERT   Serves 4–6

rall timing 35 minutes plus chilling

pment 2 bowls, saucepan, glass
l, greaseproof paper, foil

zing Not recommended

REDIENTS

sp	Cocoa	2×15ml
	Caster sugar	125g
oints	Milk	700ml
	Egg yolks	4
	Plain flour	50g
sp	Rum	2×15ml
osp	Maraschino	2×15ml
osp	Water	4×15ml
	Trifle sponges	8

METHOD

1 In a bowl, mix the cocoa and 1oz (25g)
of the sugar. Heat the milk in a saucepan and add ¼ pint (150ml) of it to the
cocoa. Stir till well blended.

2 In another bowl, beat the egg yolks
with remaining sugar and flour.
Gradually add the remaining hot milk.
Pour into a saucepan and bring to the
boil, stirring. Cook for 2 minutes till
custard thickens.

3 Pour half of the custard back into bowl
and stir in cocoa mixture. Line a glass
bowl with greaseproof paper. Put rum,
Maraschino and water on a plate. Split
the sponges in half, then halve each one.
Dip sponges in the liquid till moist but
not soggy. Line base and sides of bowl
with half the sponges.

4 Pour in the plain custard and cover
with a layer of sponges. Pour the
chocolate custard into the mould and
cover with remaining sponges. Cover
with foil or cling film and chill for at
least 3 hours but preferably overnight.

5 Turn out on to a plate, carefully
remove greaseproof paper and decorate
with whipped fresh cream if liked.

*Below: Liqueur trifle – two custards,
and sponge soaked in Maraschino*

57

Above: Bavarois à la vanille — one of the most popular European desserts

Bavarois à la vanille

A lightly textured moulded cream dessert popular in many parts of Europe. It's not known whether it originated in Bavaria or was in fact created by a chef in that country's honour

DESSERT   Serves 4–6

Overall timing 40 minutes plus cooling and setting

Equipment 3 bowls, 2 saucepans, cup, ring mould

Freezing Open freeze in mould till firm. Remove from mould, wrap well, seal and label. Freezer life: 2 months. To use: remove wrappings, place on serving plate and thaw in fridge. Decorate

INGREDIENTS

4	Eggs	4
3oz	Caster sugar	75g
½ pint	Milk	300ml
1 teasp	Vanilla essence	5ml
1 teasp	Powdered gelatine	5ml
3 tbsp	Water	3×15ml
½ pint	Carton of double cream	284ml
2oz	Glacé cherries	50g

METHOD

1 Separate the eggs. Put the yolks and 2oz (50g) of the caster sugar in a bowl placed over a pan of hot water. Whisk till pale and frothy.

2 Warm the milk and vanilla essence in a pan, then gradually stir into yolk mixture. Strain back into pan and cook very gently, stirring frequently, for 15–20 minutes or until mixture thickens. Do not boil or the mixture will curdle. Remove from heat and allow to cool. Stir from time to time to prevent a skin forming.

3 In a cup, soak the gelatine in the water for about 5 minutes till spongy, then put cup in a pan of boiling water to dissolve gelatine. Cool slightly, then trickle into cooled custard, stirring. Chill bowl of iced water to which ice cubes have been added, stirring mixture from time to time, until thick but not set.

4 In a bowl, beat the cream till soft peaks form. Stir in remaining 1oz (25g) sugar, then fold into chilled custard mixture.

5 Whisk egg whites till stiff, then carefully fold into cream and custard mixture. Turn into wetted mould and put in fridge to set.

TO SERVE

Immerse mould up to the rim in hot water, then invert on to serving plate. Decorate around the base with glacé cherries and serve at once. Eat the same day.

Strawberry flummery

This is like a *bavarois*, but of British or Irish origin. It has a fresh summery taste because of th strawberries, though you could achieve the same thing in the dep of winter with frozen fruit

DESSERT   Serve

Overall timing 35 minutes plus chill

Equipment 3 bowls, saucepan, 1½ pi (850ml) mould or individual dishes

Freezing Put into rigid container, se label and freeze. Freezer life: 2 mont To use: thaw in fridge for 3 hours, t decorate with fresh strawberries and serve

INGREDIENTS

2 teasp	Powdered gelatine	2×5
½ pint	Milk	300
4oz	Caster sugar	125
1lb	Fresh or frozen strawberries	450
½ pint	Carton of double or whipping cream	284
2 tbsp	Sherry *or*	2×1
1 tbsp	Brandy	15m

METHOD

1 Put the gelatine in a bowl with ¼ (150ml) of the milk and leave spongy.

2 Bring remaining milk to the boil pan. Remove from heat and sti sugar. Stir milk gradually into gela mixture and leave to cool.

3 Hull the strawberries and wipe ov using fresh. Make sure frozen ones thawed. Reserve a few whole st berries for the decoration. Purée rest in a blender or press throug sieve into a bowl.

4 Beat cream in a bowl till it holds peaks, then lightly stir in sherry brandy. Lightly fold cream mix into strawberry purée.

5 As soon as the gelatine mixture st to set, lightly whisk it into the str berry and cream mixture. Pour in wetted mould or individual dish preferred and place in fridge.

6 When firm, turn out, decorate reserved strawberries and serve langue de chat biscuits.

oganberry ring mould

quick-to-prepare chilled dessert
 made from canned loganberries set in
creamy raspberry jelly. A good
mily dessert to make using some
igredients from the storecupboard

| DESSERT | | Serves 6 |

overall timing 25 minutes plus chilling

quipment 2 bowls, saucepan, 1½ pint
350ml) ring mould

reezing Open freeze in mould until firm.
emove from mould, wrap, seal and
bel. Freezer life: 2 months. To use:
move wrapping, place on serving dish
id thaw in fridge

INGREDIENTS

4½oz	Can of loganberries	411g
	Raspberry jelly tablet	1
pint	Carton of double or whipping cream	150ml
	Langue de chat biscuits	

METHOD

1 Drain loganberries, reserving syrup,
   and press through a sieve.
2 Make up jelly, using loganberry syrup
   as part of the required amount of liquid.
   Stir in sieved fruit and leave to cool and
   set slightly.
3 Whip cream and fold into mixture, then
   pour into wetted ring mould. Chill till
   firm (2–4 hours). Chill serving plate at
   the same time.
4 Dip the mould in hot water to loosen,
   turn out on to chilled serving plate and
   arrange biscuits in centre of ring just
   before serving.

Loganberry cups

Framboise, a raspberry liqueur, would
be ideal to enhance the taste of the
loganberries in this recipe. The fruit
is macerated first in sweet
white wine for even more flavour

| DESSERT | | Serves 4 |

Overall timing 30 minutes plus chilling

Equipment Large bowl, saucepan,
4 serving glasses

Freezing Not recommended

INGREDIENTS

12oz	Loganberries	350g
4 tbsp	Sweet white wine	4×15ml
2oz	Caster sugar	50g
2 tbsp	Liqueur	2×15ml
½	Lemon jelly tablet	½
1oz	Toasted chopped almonds	25g

METHOD

1 Hull and pick over loganberries. Put
   into a large bowl, pour wine over and
   leave in a cool place for 15 minutes.
2 Drain off juices and reserve. Add sugar
   and liqueur to bowl and chill in fridge
   for 1 hour.
3 Meanwhile, divide the jelly into pieces.
   Put into a pan with the reserved juice
   and stir over a low heat till dissolved.
   Allow to cool.
4 Divide loganberries between serving
   dishes. Top with jelly and toasted
   almonds. Serve chilled and topped with
   a swirl of whipped cream.

*Below: Loganberry ring mould – a colourful
jelly decorated with langue de chat biscuits*

Cinnamon fruit purée

A combination of dried fruits and apples is flavoured with cinnamon, then gently stewed and puréed to make the rich dessert. For a slightly different taste, replace ½ pint (300ml) of the soaking liquor with strained cold tea

DESSERT   Serves 4

Overall timing 1½ hours plus overnight maceration and cooling

Equipment Large bowl, saucepan, sieve or blender

Freezing Place in rigid container, leaving ½ inch (12.5mm) headspace, seal, label and freeze. Freezer life: 4 months. To use: thaw at room temperature for 3 hours or overnight in fridge

INGREDIENTS

1lb	Mixed dried fruit (figs, apricots, peaches, pears, prunes)	450g
1¾ pints	Water	1 litre
6oz	Granulated sugar	175g
2	Apples	2
2 teasp	Ground cinnamon	2×5ml
2 tbsp	Cornflour	2×15ml
2 tbsp	Water	2×15ml

METHOD

1 Put the dried fruit in a large bowl with three-quarters of the water and the sugar and leave overnight to soak.
2 Stone the prunes. Transfer fruit to a saucepan, add remaining water and bring to the boil slowly. Cook over a low heat for about 15 minutes.
3 Peel, core and slice the apples and add with cinnamon to the pan. Cook for a further 45 minutes.
4 Drain fruit and return liquid to the pan. Push fruit through a sieve or blend for 1–2 minutes to a purée, then return to the pan.
5 Mix cornflour with 2 tbsp (2×15ml) cold water in a bowl, then stir into fruit mixture. Bring to the boil and boil for 5 minutes, stirring, until thick, then remove from heat and allow to cool.
6 Pour into individual serving glasses and chill for 2 hours before serving.

Right: Cinnamon fruit purée – serve chilled with crisp fan wafers

uscat trifle

e sweetness and full-bodied flavour
muscat wine makes it an excellent
dition both to plain cakes and to
n desserts such as this. The trifle
ssembled in layers, then topped
h a syllabub mixture

SSERT Serves 6

erall timing 1¾ hours including
lling

iipment 4 bowls, deep glass serving
n, whisk

ezing Not recommended

GREDIENTS

	Orange	1
z	Caster sugar	125g
int	Muscat wine	150ml
z	Muscat grapes	225g
	Large peaches	3
z	Sponge cake crumbs	125g
int	Carton of double cream	284ml
	Egg whites	2
	Chocolate curls	

THOD

Wash the orange and grate the rind
into a bowl. Add the sugar and all but
2 tbsp (2×15ml) of the wine and stir
till the sugar dissolves. Squeeze the
juice from the orange into another
bowl, add the remaining muscat wine
and reserve.
Wash and halve the grapes. Wash and
halve the peaches and discard the
stones. Remove the skins, if liked. Slice
the peaches thinly and mix with the
grapes. Spread half over the base of the
serving dish.
Sprinkle the cake crumbs over and
then the reserved orange juice mixture.
Cover with the remaining mixed fruit
and smooth the top.
Whisk the cream in a large bowl till it
holds its shape. Gradually fold in the
rind, wine and sugar mixture. Whisk
the egg whites till stiff and dry and fold
gently into cream with metal spoon.
Spread the cream mixture over the
fruit and cake crumbs and smooth the
top. Chill for 1 hour. Decorate the top
with chocolate curls before serving.

ARIATIONS

e strawberries, mandarines or rasp-
rries, or a combination of fresh fruit,
tead of peaches. Vary the taste and
ture of the trifle by using crusted maca-
ons or ratafias, or thin slices of swiss roll.

Blackberry and butter cream rings

Light and crisp rings that make a
mouth-watering dessert, or
something special to serve at tea-time

DESSERT Makes 20

Overall timing 45 minutes

Equipment 2–3 baking trays, heavy-
based saucepan, piping bag and ½ inch
(12.5mm) fluted nozzle, bowl

Freezing Pack unfilled rings into
polythene bag. Seal, label and freeze.
Freezer life: 6 months. To use: thaw in
wrapping at room temperature for
1 hour before splitting and filling. For
crisper rings, refresh in moderate oven
for 5–10 minutes after thawing, then
cool and fill

INGREDIENTS

	Rings	
5oz	Plain flour	150g
½ pint	Water	300ml
	Pinch of salt	
4oz	Butter	125g
3–4	Eggs	3–4
	Filling	
8oz	Blackberries	225g
3 tbsp	Icing sugar	3×15ml
¾ pint	Double cream	400ml
½ teasp	Vanilla essence	2.5ml
	Icing sugar	

METHOD

1 Preheat oven to 425F (220C) Gas 7.
Grease baking trays. Sieve the flour.
2 Slowly heat the water, salt and butter
together in a saucepan. When butter
has melted quickly bring liquid to the
boil then remove from heat.
3 Add the flour all at once to the pan and
beat until the dough is smooth and
leaves the sides of the pan cleanly.
Leave for a while to cool slightly.
4 Mix in 3 eggs one at a time, beating
well after each addition. Don't add the
4th egg if the batter falls from the
spoon in soft drops.
5 Put the batter into a piping bag and
pipe 10 "figure of 8's" on to baking
trays. Place in oven towards the top
and bake for 20–25 minutes until
crisp. Do not open the oven door during
the first 10 minutes as this will cause
the rings to fall.
6 Wash and dry blackberries and sprinkle
with 2 tbsp (2×15ml) of the icing sugar.

Above: Blackberry and cream rings

7 Lift rings off baking trays and place on
wire rack to cool. Make two rings of
each "8", then slice them horizontally.
Whip cream with remaining icing
sugar and vanilla essence. Spoon into
piping bag and pipe swirls on to half
the rings. Top with blackberries, then
cover with the other rings. Dust rings
with a little icing sugar before serving.

shape saver

The weight conscious need not be
denied these delicious rings. They
taste equally splendid if filled with a
thick apple purée mixed with finely
grated lemon rind and freshly
picked blackberries.

Kumquat and melon baskets

Above: Kumquat and melon baskets – ser this colourful selection of fruits with ice cream to end a summer dinner party

An attractively presented and refreshing dessert of fresh and preserved fruits macerated in Kirsch or other liqueur, then served chilled

DESSERT   Serves 4

Overall timing 20 minutes plus chilling

Equipment Sharp knife, melon baller

Freezing Not recommended

INGREDIENTS

4	Small melons	4
12	Fresh or canned lychees	12
6–8	Candied or fresh kumquats	6–8
12	Glacé cherries	12
4 tbsp	Kirsch or other fruit liqueur	4×15ml

METHOD

1 Using a sharp knife, cut out top third of melons in a zigzag shape creating a handle to each basket at the same time.
2 Remove seeds and scoop out most of the flesh with a melon baller or knife to leave room for the other fruit.
3 Put pieces of melon in a bowl with peeled, halved and stoned lychees, quartered kumquats and cherries. Sprinkle with Kirsch and mix well.
4 Pile mixture into melon baskets and chill in fridge for at least 1 hour before serving with vanilla ice cream.

HOME-PRESERVED KUMQUATS

Wash 1lb (450g) fresh kumquats. Prick fruit with a fork and make a cross in the top of each with a knife. Bring $\frac{1}{2}$ pint (300ml) water, 8oz (225g) sugar and 4 tbsp (4×15ml) honey to boil in a saucepan. Add fruit and cook over a low heat till almost transparent. The juice should be thick and syrupy. Pour into clean, warm, screw-top jars. Screw on lids and allow to cool. Leave for at least 2 months before serving as a dessert with cream.

Cherries in syrup

Cherries only have a very short season and this recipe brings out the best in the fresh fruit. The made-up dish also freezes well for eating at other times of the year

DESSERT   Serves 4

Overall timing   30 minutes, plus 1 hour chilling time

Equipment   Saucepan, 4 glass serving dishes

Freezing   Pack in rigid container leaving ½ inch (12.5mm) headspace. Freezer life: 12 months. To use: thaw at room temperature for 4 hours

INGREDIENTS

1¾lb	Red cherries	750g
7oz	Caster sugar	200g
18fl oz	Bottle of red wine	500ml
¼ pint	Water	150ml
	Small stick of cinnamon bark	
½	Orange	½
1 tbsp	Arrowroot	15ml
	Sponge fingers	

METHOD

1. Wash and dry the cherries. Remove stalks and stones. Put cherries into a saucepan with the sugar, all but 2 tbsp (2×15ml) of the wine, water, cinnamon bark and the thinly pared zest of the orange.
2. Bring to the boil, stirring. Simmer for 10 minutes. Mix arrowroot with reserved wine, stir into cherries and cook for a few minutes till syrup is clear.
3. Cool, then chill for at least 1 hour.
4. Remove the cinnamon stick and orange zest from the cherries. Spoon into individual dishes.

TO SERVE

Sponge fingers or crisp crêpes dentelles are a delicious accompaniment to this dessert, with a dish of lightly whipped, unsweetened cream.

Spicy cheese dessert

Cream cheese, spiced and then pressed to remove excess moisture, is a simple dessert, easily made at home. A sieve can be used instead of a perforated mould, or make 4 individual portions by dividing the mixture between 4 yogurt or cream cartons with holes punched in the bottom

DESSERT   Serves 4

Overall timing   10 minutes plus overnight draining

Equipment   Mixing bowl, pierced metal, china or earthenware mould or a metal sieve, muslin cloth

Freezing   Not recommended

INGREDIENTS

8oz	Cream cheese	225g
¼ teasp	Ground mace	1.25ml
¼ teasp	Ground cloves	1.25ml
¼ teasp	Freshly-grated nutmeg	1.25ml
¼ teasp	Salt	1.25ml
1 tbsp	Caster sugar	15ml
¼ pint	Carton of single cream	150ml

METHOD

1. Put cream cheese in a mixing bowl and work in the spices, salt and sugar. If it is very dry, add a little cream or milk.
2. Wet a piece of muslin in cold water and wring it out. Line mould or sieve with muslin and press the cheese into it.
3. Place the mould on a plate and leave cheese to drain overnight.
4. The next day, turn out the cheese on to a serving dish and pour over the cream. Have to hand extra caster sugar for sprinkling over the cream if wanted.

Left: Cherries in syrup, fresh cherries in cinnamon-flavoured wine

Irish lemon pudding

A moist, luscious sponge mixture with a golden brown sugar topping

DESSERT   Serves 4–6

Overall timing 1 hour

Equipment 7 inch (18cm) soufflé dish, 2 bowls, roasting tin

Freezing Not recommended

INGREDIENTS

4oz	Butter	125g
6oz	Caster sugar	175g
4	Eggs	4
1	Lemon	1
3 tbsp	Plain flour	3×15ml
½ pint	Milk	300ml
1 tbsp	Icing sugar	15ml

METHOD

1 Preheat the oven to 400F (200C) Gas 6. Grease soufflé dish.
2 Cream the butter and sugar in a bowl till light and fluffy. Separate the eggs and add the yolks to the creamed mixture. Beat well.
3 Grate rind from lemon and squeeze out juice. Beat into the creamed mixture. Gradually stir in the flour, then the milk.
4 Beat egg whites till stiff, then carefully fold into mixture. Turn into prepared soufflé dish and sift icing sugar over.
5 Place dish in roasting tin containing 1 inch (2.5cm) hot water. Bake in the centre of the oven for 40–50 minutes till the pudding has risen and the top is golden. Serve cold.

Below: Irish lemon pudding – serve it on its own, or top with a fresh raspberry or strawberry sauce for extra flavour

Cream the butter and sugar until light and fluffy, then beat in egg yolks. Grate lemon rind and squeeze out juice; add both to bowl

When the rind and juice have been beaten into the creamed mixture, gradually stir in the flour using a figure-of-eight motion

Continue to stir in flour making sure all lumps are removed, then stir in the milk a little at a time to obtain a smooth mixture

Beat egg whites till stiff, then carefully fold into creamed mixture. Turn into the prepared dish and sift icing sugar over

...ackcurrant ...arlotte

...e's no cooking involved in
...ing this dessert, which is a
...bination of fresh fruit and
... and sponge fingers which are
...tened with liqueur. It's a
... to serve on a special
...sion because it can be made
... in advance

...ERT		Serves 8

...all timing 30 minutes plus
...night chilling

...oment 2 bowls, 6 inch (15cm)
...-bottom cake tin or charlotte mould

...ing Freeze charlotte while still in
...ld. Turn out when frozen and store,
...ped in foil. Freezer life: 2 months.
...se: leave overnight in fridge.
...rate before serving

...REDIENTS

	Blackcurrants	125g
	Caster sugar	50g
p	Kirsch or Cointreau	3×15ml
t	Water	150ml
	Sponge fingers	40
t	Carton of double cream	284ml
	Icing sugar	50g
	Jar of blackcurrant jam	227g

...HOD
...p and tail blackcurrants, then wash
...der running water in a sieve. Place
... a bowl and sprinkle over caster sugar.
...ix Kirsch or Cointreau and water in
...bowl. Quickly dip the sponge fingers
...e at a time into the liquid without
...aking them. Use about 8 fingers to
...e the base of the cake tin or charlotte
...ould, and about 20 round the sides.
...im if sponges come above the top
...ge of the tin.
...hip the cream with the icing sugar
...til stiff, then fill the mould with
...ternate layers of blackcurrant jam,
...onge fingers, sugared blackcurrants
...d whipped cream. Reserve some
... the whipped cream and black-
...rrants for decoration.
...ver the charlotte with a plate, place
...weight on top and chill for 12 hours
... overnight.
...hen ready to serve, turn the charlotte
...t on to a serving plate and decorate
...ith remaining whipped cream and
...ackcurrants.

Above: Malaga dessert — quick to prepare with creamy cheese and lightly chilled

Malaga dessert

Soft cream cheese is combined with
raisins — which come from Malaga
grapes, hence the name. For best
results, make just before serving.

DESSERT		Serves 4

Overall timing 35 minutes

Equipment Saucepan, 2 bowls, 4
stemmed glasses

Freezing Not recommended

INGREDIENTS

3oz	Raisins	75g
1 tbsp	Water	15ml
2 tbsp	Rum	2×15ml
3oz	Flaked almonds	75g
12oz	Cream cheese	350g
3 tbsp	Caster sugar	3×15ml

METHOD
1 Put raisins and water in a pan, cover
and heat for a few minutes until the
water has evaporated. Remove lid and
gently heat a little more until raisins
are plump and dry. Put into small bowl
with rum and leave for 15 minutes.
2 Meanwhile, toast almonds under a hot
grill till golden.
3 Put the cheese, sugar and rum (drained
from the raisins) into a bowl and beat
till light and fluffy. Mix in raisins and
two-thirds of the toasted almonds.
4 Divide mixture between serving glasses
and sprinkle remaining almonds on
top. Chill for 10–15 minutes before
serving – not longer or the texture will
be too firm.

VARIATION
To give a really pretty effect for a special
occasion, cut 2 oranges in half by making
deep zig-zag cuts to the centre right round
the middle of each fruit. Remove flesh with
a grapefruit knife and fill shells with
cheese and raisin mixture, adding almonds.

Cassata alla siciliana

A magnificently rich and sweet gâteau made with Ricotta and not ice cream as the name suggests. Use cream cheese instead if liked

DESSERT Cuts into 8

Overall timing 1 hour plus overnight chilling

Equipment 8½ inch (21cm) springform or round loose-bottomed cake tin, greaseproof paper, 2 saucepans, sieve, bowl

Freezing Open freeze, then pack in rigid container. Cover and label. Freezer life: 1 month. To use: remove from container and thaw at room temperature

INGREDIENTS

1	Sponge cake	1
6oz	Apricot jam	175g
2 tbsp	Maraschino	2×15ml
	Filling	
1lb	Ricotta	450g
8oz	Caster sugar	225g
3fl oz	Water	90ml
8oz	Mixed glacé fruit	225g
3½oz	Plain dessert chocolate	100g
1oz	Shelled unsalted pistachios or pine nuts	25g
2 tbsp	Maraschino	2×15ml
	Decoration	
	Apricot glaze	
2oz	Icing sugar	50g
2oz	Mixed glacé fruits (pineapple chunks, cherries, apricots, angelica)	50g
8	Fresh black cherries	8

METHOD

1 Cut cake into ½ inch (12.5mm) thick slices. Line base and sides of tin with greaseproof paper, then with slices of cake, trimmed to size. Reserve remaining cake.

2 In a saucepan, mix apricot jam with Maraschino. Bring to the boil, then press through a sieve. Use a little of the mixture to bind the cake slices together. Reserve remainder for decoration.

3 To make the filling, mix Ricotta in a bowl with a wooden spoon until smooth. Put the caster sugar in a pan

with the water. Dissolve over gentle heat, stirring from time to time, then bring to the boil and cook until the syrup thickens and begins to change colour. Remove from heat and whisk syrup into Ricotta.

4 Add the chopped glacé fruits, grated chocolate and finely chopped pistachios or pine nuts. Mix well with a wooden spoon and stir in the Maraschino.

5 Carefully pour into the prepared tin to within ½ inch (12.5mm) of the top and smooth over surface. Cover with reserved slices of cake, then chill in fridge overnight.

6 The next day, put remaining apricot glaze and icing sugar in a pan. Cook over a low heat, stirring all the time, till syrupy.

7 Remove cassata from fridge, turn out on to serving plate and carefully remove greaseproof paper. Spoon apricot glaze over the top and sides of the cassata and spread with a wetted palette knife.

8 Decorate with glacé fruit and fresh cherries and chill till ready to serve.

Champagne fruit salad

A fruit salad for a festive occasion. It gains in flavour from the distinctive bouquet of champagne. As an alternative use cider — it blends well with fruit because it's apple based

Above: Cassata alla siciliana — as rich on the outside as it is on the inside

DESSERT Serve

Overall timing 15 minutes plus chill

Equipment Saucepan, melon baller, serving bowl

Freezing As Liqueur, right

INGREDIENTS

4oz	Caster sugar	125g
¼ pint	Water	150m
2	Apples	2
3	Mandarines	3
½	Pineapple	½
1	Banana	1
2oz	Green grapes	50g
¼ pint	Champagne or sparkling cider	150m

METHOD

1 Put the sugar and water in a pan. over a gentle heat till the s dissolves. Remove from heat and aside.

2 Peel and core apples. Shape with a melon baller, or cut into chu Peel mandarines and divide into ments. Peel pineapple and cut chunks. Peel and slice banana. grapes. Put prepared fruit into ser bowl.

3 Stir champagne into cooled sy Ladle over fruit and mix well. for at least 1 hour before serving.

...eel and core apples and remove flesh...melon baller, or cut into chunks

...ivide mandarines carefully into...ents, removing all the pith

...tir the champagne or cider into...ooled syrup

...adle syrup mixture over the fruit....thoroughly and chill before serving

Above: Liqueur fruit salad – a simple to make, refreshingly different finish to a meal

Liqueur fruit salad

The addition of liqueur makes this a special dish for a dinner party

DESSERT   Serves 4

Overall timing 15 minutes plus chilling

Equipment Bowl

Freezing Cover fruit with syrup in a rigid container. Cover, label and freeze. Freezer life: 3 months. To use: thaw overnight in fridge

INGREDIENTS

2lb	Mixed fresh fruit	900g
1	Lemon	1
1	Orange	1
4 tbsp	Caster sugar	4×15ml
3 tbsp	Curaçao or Grand Marnier	3×15ml

METHOD
1 Wash and prepare fruit, cutting into small chunks as necessary, and put into a bowl.
2 Pare away a small strip of lemon rind and add to bowl. Squeeze juice from lemon and orange and add to fruit with the sugar and liqueur. Mix carefully without damaging the fruit.
3 Cover and chill for 2–3 hours. Remove lemon rind and serve with whipped cream and crisp biscuits.

Nutty fruit salad

Toasted nuts add a delicious crunchiness to this fruit salad

DESSERT   Serves 6

Overall timing 20 minutes plus chilling

Equipment Saucepan, large bowl

Freezing As Liqueur, left

INGREDIENTS

4oz	Caster sugar	125g
½ pint	Water	300ml
2	Apples, bananas, pears, mandarines	2
3	Oranges	3
½	Pineapple	½
4oz	Toasted nuts	125g
4oz	Alpine strawberries	125g
	Grated rind of ½ lemon	
4 tbsp	Maraschino or Cherry brandy	4×15ml

METHOD
1 Put sugar and water in a saucepan. Stir over a low heat till the sugar dissolves and forms a syrup. Remove from heat.
2 Prepare fruit, except 1 orange. Put prepared fruit into a large bowl.
3 Add toasted nuts, washed and hulled strawberries and lemon rind.
4 Pour syrup over. Squeeze juice from remaining orange and add to bowl with Maraschino. Mix well, cover and chill.

Cold strawberry soufflé

An elegant and impressive dessert to end a summer dinner party. It can be made the day before and the finishing touches quickly done at the last minute

DESSERT   Serves 6

Overall timing 45 minutes plus chilling

Equipment 5 inch (13cm) soufflé dish, greaseproof paper or foil, 3 bowls, sieve

Freezing Use foil not greaseproof for collar. Open freeze undecorated soufflé till firm, wrap in polythene bag, seal and label. Freezer life: 2 months. To use: leave collar on and thaw overnight in fridge or for 4 hours at room temperature. Decorate with fresh cream and fruit

INGREDIENTS

4 tbsp	Water	4×15ml
2 tbsp	Powdered gelatine	2×15ml
2lb	Strawberries	900g
6oz	Caster sugar	175g
2	Lemons	2
3	Egg whites	3
½ pint	Carton of double cream	284ml

METHOD

1 Tie a collar of double greaseproof paper or foil round the outside of the soufflé dish 2 inches (5cm) above rim.
2 Put the water into a bowl, sprinkle gelatine over and leave to sponge.
3 Wash and hull strawberries, reserve 7 or so for decoration and sieve the rest.
4 Put half the fruit purée into a pan with the gelatine and the sugar. Squeeze juice from lemons and add. Stir over a gentle heat until sugar and gelatine dissolve. Remove from heat and stir in the remaining fruit purée. Leave to cool.

5 Whisk the egg whites till stiff. In an[other] bowl, whisk the cream till stiff. [Fold] all but 3 tbsp (3×15ml) of the c[ream] into the whites. Turn into prep[ared] dish and chill until firm.

TO SERVE

Carefully remove collar. If you like, sti[r] (50g) finely chopped almonds and a [few] drops of green food colouring together[,] press on to the exposed edges of the so[ufflé] with a palette knife. Decorate with[the] reserved cream and halved strawbe[rries.]

Tipsy blackberries

A treat for those who like Advocat and cherry brandy

DESSERT   Serv[es]

Overall timing 30 minutes

Equipment 2 bowls

Freezing Not recommended

INGREDIENTS

12oz	Blackberries	350g
3 tbsp	Caster sugar	3×1[5ml]
4fl oz	Cherry brandy	120m[l]
½ pint	Carton of double cream	284[ml]
¼ pint	Carton of single cream	150m[l]
4fl oz	Advocat liqueur	120m[l]
1oz	Crushed praline	25g

METHOD

1 Wash blackberries and set aside a [few] for decoration. Place the rest in a b[owl,] sprinkle with sugar and pour on [the] cherry brandy. Leave for 20 min[utes.] Place serving dish in fridge to chi[ll.]
2 Whip creams together in chilled [bowl.] Fold in soaked blackberries, then [pour] liqueur over and sprinkle with pra[line.] Decorate with blackberries and s[erve.]

Left: Cold strawberry soufflé – a light foam mix decorated with rosettes of crea[m,] strawberries and coloured chopped nuts.

Baked coffee caramel ring

A variation on the theme of the much appreciated crème caramel. The added coffee and liqueur or brandy gives the custard a slightly darker colour and delicious flavour. The custard is baked in a bain-marie to slow down the cooking and prevent bubbles forming in the mixture

DESSERT	Serves 6

Overall timing 2 hours plus cooling and overnight chilling

Equipment 2 saucepans, pastry brush, 3 pint (1.7 litre) mould with funnel, bowl

Freezing Not recommended

INGREDIENTS

7oz	Caster sugar	200g
¼ pint	Water	150ml
8	Eggs	8
1¾ pints	Milk	1 litre
¼ pint	Strong black coffee	150ml
3 tbsp	Tia Maria or brandy	3×15ml

METHOD

1 Put all but 4 tbsp (4×15ml) of the sugar into a saucepan with the water and stir over a low heat till the sugar dissolves. Wash any sugar crystals on the sides of the pan into the syrup with a pastry brush dipped in cold water.

2 Stop stirring and bring to the boil. Boil steadily till a deep golden brown. Pour into the mould, turning it so the base and sides are coated with caramel.

3 Preheat the oven to 325F (170C) Gas 3. Put the eggs and remaining sugar into a large bowl and whisk together lightly. Put the milk into a pan and heat till almost boiling, then pour in the coffee and stir well.

4 Pour on to the eggs in a thin stream, whisking constantly. Add the Tia Maria or brandy, then strain the custard into the caramel-lined mould.

5 Stand the mould in a roasting tin containing 1½ inches (4cm) hot water. Cover the mould with foil and bake in the centre of the oven for about 1¼ hours till custard is set.

6 Remove from the oven and leave to cool completely. Chill overnight.

7 To turn out custard, place mould on the table and put a deepish serving dish over it. Hold the dish and mould together and turn them over. Put the dish on the table and lift off the mould carefully. Serve immediately with whipped cream and crisp biscuits.

VARIATION

To make individual custards, line each mould with caramel, then divide custard between them. Cover each mould with foil and place in roasting tin with ½ inch (12.5mm) hot water. Bake at 350F (180C) Gas 4 for 45 minutes till custards are set. Chill overnight, turn out to serve.

The milk is heated till almost boiling, then the black coffee is stirred in well

The milk/coffee is whisked into beaten eggs/sugar, placed in caramel-lined mould

After baking and overnight chilling, the set custard and runny caramel is unmoulded

Left: Baked coffee caramel ring — superb tasting dessert to serve with cream

Loganberries in liqueur

In Europe, the spirit used is *eau de vie*, which is flavourless. As it is not normally available elsewhere, this recipe uses gin or vodka

DESSERT   Makes 1¾ pints (1 litre)

Overall timing 15 minutes plus maceration

Equipment Sterilized wide-necked airtight jars

Freezing Not recommended

INGREDIENTS

2½lb	Loganberries	1.1kg
12oz	Caster sugar	350g
1¾ pints	Gin or vodka	1 litre

METHOD

1 Hull and pick over loganberries. Place layers of loganberries and sugar in the jars, making sure they are full. Pour over spirit, seal and leave in a sunny place if possible for a few days.
2 Transfer the jars to a cool place and store for 2–3 months before serving with whipped cream.

Below: Loganberries in liqueur – a most delightful dessert to serve with cream

Mousse Amaretto

A gelatine-set custard mousse flavoured with Amaretto di Saronno and served in glasses with the liqueur poured over

DESSERT   Serves 8

Overall timing 30 minutes plus chilling

Equipment 4 bowls, 2 saucepans

Freezing Open freeze till firm. Overwrap seal, label and freeze. Freezer life: 3 months. To use: unwrap and thaw for 6 hours in fridge

INGREDIENTS

5	Eggs	5
4oz	Caster sugar	125g
	Salt	
8fl oz	Milk	220ml
1	Vanilla pod	1
1 tbsp	Powdered gelatine	15ml
2 tbsp	Cold water	2×15ml
1 pint	Double cream	560ml
7 tbsp	Amaretto di Saronno	7×15ml

METHOD

1 Separate the eggs. Beat the yolks in bowl with the sugar till pale and thick Add a pinch of salt.
2 Bring milk and vanilla pod to boil in saucepan, then remove pod. Whisk h milk into yolk mixture, then strain bac into pan and cook gently, stirrin continuously, until the mixtur thickens and will coat the back of th spoon. Remove from heat.
3 Sprinkle the gelatine on to the co water in a small bowl and leave t sponge. Place the bowl in a pan simmering water and stir till dissolve Allow to cool slightly, then trickle into the custard in a thin strean stirring constantly. Chill until begir ning to set.
4 Whip cream in a bowl till stiff, the fold into chilled custard mixture.
5 Whisk egg whites till stiff but not dr and fold into the custard mixture wit a metal spoon. Gently fold in 4 tbs (4×15ml) of the Amaretto. Divid between individual serving dishes glasses and chill in fridge for at lea 3 hours.

TO SERVE

Divide remaining Amaretto between eac serving of the mousse – just pour it ove

weet flan pastry

fragile but delicious pastry
t marks any flan as French.
s also known as *paté sablée*

erall timing 1¾ hours including
lling time

uipment Large bowl, rolling-pin,
ch (23cm) flan ring or dish
8 small rings)

ezing To freeze pastry, wrap closely
oil or cling film, label with quantity,
d and freeze. Freezer life: 3 months.
use: thaw at room temperature for
ours. To freeze cooked cases: open
ze, then pack in rigid container.
er and label. Freezer life: 6 months.
use: thaw for 3 hours, then fill

GREDIENTS

Plain flour		175g
Caster sugar		75g
Salt		
Softened butter		100g
Egg yolks		2

METHOD

1 In a large bowl, place flour, sugar, pinch of salt and butter cut into small pieces.
2 Work the mixture between the fingers and palms of your hands until the mixture resembles fine crumbs.
3 Add egg yolks and work them into the mixture very quickly with your hand. When the pastry no longer sticks to your fingers, shape it into a ball, wrap and place in fridge for 1 hour.
4 Preheat oven to 400F (200C) Gas 6.
5 Roll out the pastry to ¼ inch (6mm) thickness with the rolling-pin on a lightly-floured board. Line flan ring, dish or small pans to make tartlets. Prick the base with a fork and bake blind (either line with greaseproof paper and baking beans, or with foil pressed closely to the pastry). Cook flan for 10 minutes (tartlets 5 minutes) towards top of oven. Remove lining and beans and cook for further 5–10 minutes till lightly golden. Because of the high sugar content, the cooking time is shorter than sweet shortcrust.
6 To prevent breakage, let flan cool in the ring or dish before being turned on to a serving dish and filled. Turn out small pastry cases while still hot.

Crème pâtissière

French chefs who specialize in pastries and sweet confections are called pâtissiers – hence this name

FILLING   Makes 1 pint (560ml)

Overall timing 20 minutes plus cooling

Equipment Saucepan, bowl, fine sieve

Freezing Not recommended

INGREDIENTS

1 pint	Milk	560ml
	Pinch of salt	
1	Vanilla pod	1
	Strip of lemon rind	
8 tbsp	Caster sugar	8×15ml
4	Medium eggs	4
4 tbsp	Plain flour	4×15ml

METHOD

1 Put the milk, salt, vanilla pod and lemon rind into a pan and bring to the boil. Remove from heat and leave to infuse for 10 minutes.
2 Beat the sugar and eggs in a bowl, then stir in the flour and beat till smooth.
3 Remove vanilla pod and lemon rind. Gradually stir milk into bowl. Strain mixture back into saucepan and slowly bring back to the boil. Cook, stirring constantly, for 2–4 minutes or until thick.
4 Remove from heat. Cover with damp greaseproof paper to prevent skin forming. Leave to cool before using.

tter is cut into chunks and added the dry ingredients in bowl

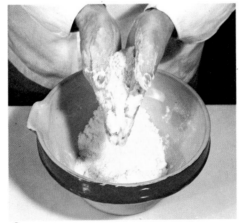

The mixture is worked between the fingers till it resembles breadcrumbs

yolks instead of water are used to the other ingredients

Mix the yolks in by hand or with a spoon, for a firm, not-sticky consistency

Index